C000126877

Workload Security Capabilities
Complete Self-Assessment Guide

The guidance in this Self-Assessment is based on Workload Security
Capabilities best practices and standards in business process
architecture, design and quality management. The guidance is also based
on the professional judgment of the individual collaborators listed in the
Acknowledgments.

Notice of rights

**You are licensed to use the Self-Assessment contents in your
presentations and materials for internal use and customers
without asking us - we are here to help.**

Trademarks

Table of Contents

About The Art of Service

The Art of Service, Business Process Architects since 2000, is dedicated to helping stakeholders achieve excellence.

Defining, designing, creating, and implementing a process to solve a stakeholders challenge or meet an objective is the most valuable role… In EVERY group, company, organization and department.

Unless you're talking a one-time, single-use project, there should be a process. Whether that process is managed and implemented by humans, AI, or a combination of the two, it needs to be designed by someone with a complex enough perspective to ask the right questions.

Someone capable of asking the right questions and step back and say, 'What are we really trying to accomplish here? And is there a different way to look at it?'

With The Art of Service's Standard Requirements Self-Assessments, we empower people who can do just that — whether their title is marketer, entrepreneur, manager, salesperson, consultant, Business Process Manager, executive assistant, IT Manager, CIO etc... —they are the people who rule the future. They are people who watch the process as it happens, and ask the right questions to make the process work better.

Contact us when you need any support with this Self-Assessment and any help with templates, blue-prints and examples of standard documents you might need:

http://theartofservice.com
service@theartofservice.com

Included Resources - how to access

Included with your purchase of the book is the Workload

Security Capabilities Self-Assessment Spreadsheet Dashboard which contains all questions and Self-Assessment areas and auto-generates insights, graphs, and project RACI planning - all with examples to get you started right away.

How? Simply send an email to
access@theartofservice.com
with this books' title in the subject to get the Workload Security Capabilities Self Assessment Tool right away.

You will receive the following contents with New and Updated specific criteria:

- The latest quick edition of the book in PDF

- The latest complete edition of the book in PDF, which criteria correspond to the criteria in...

- The Self-Assessment Excel Dashboard, and...

- Example pre-filled Self-Assessment Excel Dashboard to get familiar with results generation

- In-depth specific Checklists covering the topic

- Project management checklists and templates to assist with implementation

Purpose of this Self-Assessment

This Self-Assessment has been developed to improve understanding of the requirements and elements of Workload Security Capabilities, based on best practices and standards in business process architecture, design and quality management.

It is designed to allow for a rapid Self-Assessment to determine how closely existing management practices and procedures correspond to the elements of the Self-Assessment.

The criteria of requirements and elements of Workload Security Capabilities have been rephrased in the format of a Self-Assessment questionnaire, with a seven-criterion scoring system, as explained in this document.

In this format, even with limited background knowledge of Workload Security Capabilities, a manager can quickly review existing operations to determine how they measure up to the standards. This in turn can serve as the starting point of a 'gap analysis' to identify management tools or system elements that might usefully be implemented in the organization to help improve overall performance.

How to use the Self-Assessment

On the following pages are a series of questions to identify to what extent your Workload Security Capabilities initiative is complete in comparison to the requirements set in standards.

To facilitate answering the questions, there is a space in front of each question to enter a score on a scale of '1' to '5'.

1 Strongly Disagree

2 Disagree

3 Neutral

4 Agree

5 Strongly Agree

Read the question and rate it with the following in front of mind:

'In my belief,
the answer to this question is clearly defined'.

There are two ways in which you can choose to interpret this statement;
1. how aware are you that the answer to the question is clearly defined
2. for more in-depth analysis you can choose to gather evidence and confirm the answer to the question. This obviously will take more time, most Self-Assessment users opt for the first way to interpret the question and dig deeper later on based on the outcome of the overall Self-Assessment.

A score of '1' would mean that the answer is not clear at all, where a '5' would mean the answer is crystal clear and defined. Leave emtpy when the question is not applicable or you don't want to answer it, you can skip it without affecting your score. Write your score in the space provided.

After you have responded to all the appropriate statements in each section, compute your average score for that section, using the formula provided, and round to the nearest tenth. Then transfer to the corresponding spoke in the Workload Security Capabilities Scorecard on the second next page of the Self-Assessment.

Your completed Workload Security Capabilities Scorecard will give you a clear presentation of which Workload Security Capabilities areas need attention.

Workload Security Capabilities Scorecard Example

Example of how the finalized Scorecard can look like:

RECOGNIZE

SUSTAIN

DEFINE

CONTROL

MEASURE

IMPROVE

ANALYZE

Workload Security Capabilities Scorecard

Your Scores:

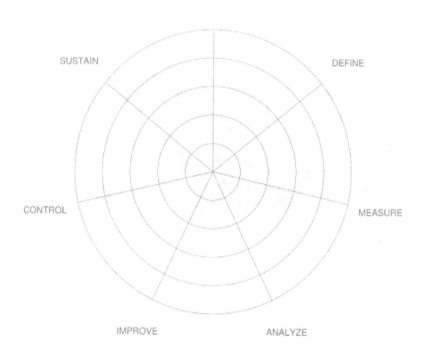

BEGINNING OF THE SELF-ASSESSMENT:

CRITERION #1: RECOGNIZE

INTENT: Be aware of the need for change. Recognize that there is an unfavorable variation, problem or symptom.

In my belief, the answer to this question is clearly defined:

5 Strongly Agree

4 Agree

3 Neutral

2 Disagree

1 Strongly Disagree

1. Who are your key stakeholders who need to sign off?
<--- Score

2. Will Workload Security Capabilities deliverables need to be tested and, if so, by whom?
<--- Score

3. Do you need to avoid or amend any Workload

Security Capabilities activities?
<--- Score

4. Can management personnel recognize the monetary benefit of Workload Security Capabilities?
<--- Score

5. What tools and technologies are needed for a custom Workload Security Capabilities project?
<--- Score

6. Which issues are too important to ignore?
<--- Score

7. What are the clients issues and concerns?
<--- Score

8. To what extent does each concerned units management team recognize Workload Security Capabilities as an effective investment?
<--- Score

9. Are there recognized Workload Security Capabilities problems?
<--- Score

10. How does it fit into your organizational needs and tasks?
<--- Score

11. What prevents you from making the changes you know will make you a more effective Workload Security Capabilities leader?
<--- Score

12. Is it clear when you think of the day ahead of you

what activities and tasks you need to complete?
<--- Score

13. What are the minority interests and what amount of minority interests can be recognized?
<--- Score

14. Are you dealing with any of the same issues today as yesterday? What can you do about this?
<--- Score

15. What Workload Security Capabilities coordination do you need?
<--- Score

16. How are the Workload Security Capabilities's objectives aligned to the group's overall stakeholder strategy?
<--- Score

17. What are the timeframes required to resolve each of the issues/problems?
<--- Score

18. Are employees recognized or rewarded for performance that demonstrates the highest levels of integrity?
<--- Score

19. When a Workload Security Capabilities manager recognizes a problem, what options are available?
<--- Score

20. What do employees need in the short term?
<--- Score

21. What is the problem and/or vulnerability?
<--- Score

22. What is the recognized need?
<--- Score

23. What Workload Security Capabilities problem should be solved?
<--- Score

24. Are there regulatory / compliance issues?
<--- Score

25. Where do you need to exercise leadership?
<--- Score

26. What should be considered when identifying available resources, constraints, and deadlines?
<--- Score

27. Who needs to know?
<--- Score

28. What problems are you facing and how do you consider Workload Security Capabilities will circumvent those obstacles?
<--- Score

29. For your Workload Security Capabilities project, identify and describe the business environment, is there more than one layer to the business environment?
<--- Score

30. Do you know what you need to know about

Workload Security Capabilities?
<--- Score

31. What are the Workload Security Capabilities resources needed?
<--- Score

32. Have you identified your Workload Security Capabilities key performance indicators?
<--- Score

33. What information do users need?
<--- Score

34. What extra resources will you need?
<--- Score

35. Is the need for organizational change recognized?
<--- Score

36. Are there any specific expectations or concerns about the Workload Security Capabilities team, Workload Security Capabilities itself?
<--- Score

37. Is the quality assurance team identified?
<--- Score

38. Will it solve real problems?
<--- Score

39. How do you identify the kinds of information that you will need?
<--- Score

40. Are there any revenue recognition issues?

<--- Score

41. What Workload Security Capabilities capabilities do you need?
<--- Score

42. How do you take a forward-looking perspective in identifying Workload Security Capabilities research related to market response and models?
<--- Score

43. Are losses recognized in a timely manner?
<--- Score

44. What are the expected benefits of Workload Security Capabilities to the stakeholder?
<--- Score

45. How many trainings, in total, are needed?
<--- Score

46. Who defines the rules in relation to any given issue?
<--- Score

47. Are controls defined to recognize and contain problems?
<--- Score

48. Are employees recognized for desired behaviors?
<--- Score

49. What needs to be done?
<--- Score

50. Think about the people you identified for your Workload Security Capabilities project and the project responsibilities you would assign to them, what kind of training do you think they would need to perform these responsibilities effectively?
<--- Score

51. Will new equipment/products be required to facilitate Workload Security Capabilities delivery, for example is new software needed?
<--- Score

52. Does your organization need more Workload Security Capabilities education?
<--- Score

53. Would you recognize a threat from the inside?
<--- Score

54. What does Workload Security Capabilities success mean to the stakeholders?
<--- Score

55. What is the problem or issue?
<--- Score

56. Looking at each person individually – does every one have the qualities which are needed to work in this group?
<--- Score

57. What is the extent or complexity of the Workload Security Capabilities problem?
<--- Score

58. Does Workload Security Capabilities create potential expectations in other areas that need to be recognized and considered?
<--- Score

59. Are your goals realistic? Do you need to redefine your problem? Perhaps the problem has changed or maybe you have reached your goal and need to set a new one?
<--- Score

60. Who needs what information?
<--- Score

61. Do you recognize Workload Security Capabilities achievements?
<--- Score

62. What vendors make products that address the Workload Security Capabilities needs?
<--- Score

63. Are problem definition and motivation clearly presented?
<--- Score

64. How do you recognize an Workload Security Capabilities objection?
<--- Score

65. What needs to stay?
<--- Score

66. Which needs are not included or involved?
<--- Score

67. Is it needed?
<--- Score

68. Whom do you really need or want to serve?
<--- Score

69. How do you recognize an objection?
<--- Score

70. What else needs to be measured?
<--- Score

71. What situation(s) led to this Workload Security Capabilities Self Assessment?
<--- Score

72. How much are sponsors, customers, partners, stakeholders involved in Workload Security Capabilities? In other words, what are the risks, if Workload Security Capabilities does not deliver successfully?
<--- Score

73. Where is training needed?
<--- Score

74. What resources or support might you need?
<--- Score

75. As a sponsor, customer or management, how important is it to meet goals, objectives?
<--- Score

76. What do you need to start doing?
<--- Score

77. How are you going to measure success?
<--- Score

78. What is the smallest subset of the problem you can usefully solve?
<--- Score

79. What are the stakeholder objectives to be achieved with Workload Security Capabilities?
<--- Score

80. Who needs budgets?
<--- Score

81. How can auditing be a preventative security measure?
<--- Score

82. How do you identify subcontractor relationships?
<--- Score

83. What would happen if Workload Security Capabilities weren't done?
<--- Score

84. To what extent would your organization benefit from being recognized as a award recipient?
<--- Score

85. Are there Workload Security Capabilities problems defined?
<--- Score

86. Why is this needed?

<--- Score

87. Who needs to know about Workload Security Capabilities?
<--- Score

88. What is the Workload Security Capabilities problem definition? What do you need to resolve?
<--- Score

89. Who else hopes to benefit from it?
<--- Score

90. Does the problem have ethical dimensions?
<--- Score

91. Consider your own Workload Security Capabilities project, what types of organizational problems do you think might be causing or affecting your problem, based on the work done so far?
<--- Score

92. Who should resolve the Workload Security Capabilities issues?
<--- Score

93. Do you need different information or graphics?
<--- Score

94. What activities does the governance board need to consider?
<--- Score

95. How do you assess your Workload Security Capabilities workforce capability and capacity

needs, including skills, competencies, and staffing levels?
<--- Score

96. What creative shifts do you need to take?
<--- Score

97. Do you have/need 24-hour access to key personnel?
<--- Score

98. What are your needs in relation to Workload Security Capabilities skills, labor, equipment, and markets?
<--- Score

99. What Workload Security Capabilities events should you attend?
<--- Score

100. How are training requirements identified?
<--- Score

Add up total points for this section:
_ _ _ _ _ = Total points for this section

Divided by: _ _ _ _ _ _ (number of statements answered) = _ _ _ _ _ _
Average score for this section

Transfer your score to the Workload Security Capabilities Index at the beginning of the Self-Assessment.

CRITERION #2: DEFINE:

INTENT: Formulate the stakeholder problem. Define the problem, needs and objectives.

In my belief, the answer to this question is clearly defined:

5 Strongly Agree

4 Agree

3 Neutral

2 Disagree

1 Strongly Disagree

1. Who is gathering information?
<--- Score

2. How will the Workload Security Capabilities team and the group measure complete success of Workload Security Capabilities?
<--- Score

3. What are (control) requirements for Workload

Security Capabilities Information?
<--- Score

4. What is the scope?
<--- Score

5. What intelligence can you gather?
<--- Score

6. Is the team adequately staffed with the desired cross-functionality? If not, what additional resources are available to the team?
<--- Score

7. Has the direction changed at all during the course of Workload Security Capabilities? If so, when did it change and why?
<--- Score

8. How often are the team meetings?
<--- Score

9. What is in the scope and what is not in scope?
<--- Score

10. What scope to assess?
<--- Score

11. Does the team have regular meetings?
<--- Score

12. What Workload Security Capabilities requirements should be gathered?
<--- Score

13. What Workload Security Capabilities services do

you require?

<--- Score

14. Has anyone else (internal or external to the group) attempted to solve this problem or a similar one before? If so, what knowledge can be leveraged from these previous efforts?

<--- Score

15. Is it clearly defined in and to your organization what you do?

<--- Score

16. Is there a completed SIPOC representation, describing the Suppliers, Inputs, Process, Outputs, and Customers?

<--- Score

17. What gets examined?

<--- Score

18. In what way can you redefine the criteria of choice clients have in your category in your favor?

<--- Score

19. How do you build the right business case?

<--- Score

20. How do you manage changes in Workload Security Capabilities requirements?

<--- Score

21. How do you hand over Workload Security Capabilities context?

<--- Score

22. Are there any constraints known that bear on the ability to perform Workload Security Capabilities work? How is the team addressing them?
<--- Score

23. What is the scope of Workload Security Capabilities?
<--- Score

24. Is special Workload Security Capabilities user knowledge required?
<--- Score

25. Is the scope of Workload Security Capabilities defined?
<--- Score

26. What information should you gather?
<--- Score

27. Has everyone on the team, including the team leaders, been properly trained?
<--- Score

28. What is a worst-case scenario for losses?
<--- Score

29. Do you all define Workload Security Capabilities in the same way?
<--- Score

30. What was the context?
<--- Score

31. What sources do you use to gather information for a Workload Security Capabilities study?

<--- Score

32. Where can you gather more information?
<--- Score

33. Is there a clear Workload Security Capabilities case definition?
<--- Score

34. What specifically is the problem? Where does it occur? When does it occur? What is its extent?
<--- Score

35. Is the current 'as is' process being followed? If not, what are the discrepancies?
<--- Score

36. What scope do you want your strategy to cover?
<--- Score

37. Has the improvement team collected the 'voice of the customer' (obtained feedback – qualitative and quantitative)?
<--- Score

38. When are meeting minutes sent out? Who is on the distribution list?
<--- Score

39. Is scope creep really all bad news?
<--- Score

40. Does the scope remain the same?
<--- Score

41. How would you define Workload Security

Capabilities leadership?

<--- Score

42. What happens if Workload Security Capabilities's scope changes?

<--- Score

43. Scope of sensitive information?

<--- Score

44. What are the Workload Security Capabilities tasks and definitions?

<--- Score

45. Who approved the Workload Security Capabilities scope?

<--- Score

46. How do you gather Workload Security Capabilities requirements?

<--- Score

47. Has/have the customer(s) been identified?

<--- Score

48. Is there a critical path to deliver Workload Security Capabilities results?

<--- Score

49. Who is gathering Workload Security Capabilities information?

<--- Score

50. What would be the goal or target for a Workload Security Capabilities's improvement team?

<--- Score

51. Are the Workload Security Capabilities requirements testable?
<--- Score

52. Has your scope been defined?
<--- Score

53. Will a Workload Security Capabilities production readiness review be required?
<--- Score

54. What is in scope?
<--- Score

55. What are the core elements of the Workload Security Capabilities business case?
<--- Score

56. When is the estimated completion date?
<--- Score

57. What are the record-keeping requirements of Workload Security Capabilities activities?
<--- Score

58. What is the definition of Workload Security Capabilities excellence?
<--- Score

59. Is the Workload Security Capabilities scope complete and appropriately sized?
<--- Score

60. If substitutes have been appointed, have they been briefed on the Workload Security Capabilities

goals and received regular communications as to the progress to date?

<--- Score

61. Has a high-level 'as is' process map been completed, verified and validated?

<--- Score

62. Are audit criteria, scope, frequency and methods defined?

<--- Score

63. Is the work to date meeting requirements?

<--- Score

64. What is out of scope?

<--- Score

65. How do you think the partners involved in Workload Security Capabilities would have defined success?

<--- Score

66. What information do you gather?

<--- Score

67. How and when will the baselines be defined?

<--- Score

68. How do you manage scope?

<--- Score

69. What is the worst case scenario?

<--- Score

70. What is the scope of the Workload Security

Capabilities work?

<--- Score

71. How was the 'as is' process map developed, reviewed, verified and validated?

<--- Score

72. Do the problem and goal statements meet the SMART criteria (specific, measurable, attainable, relevant, and time-bound)?

<--- Score

73. Is there any additional Workload Security Capabilities definition of success?

<--- Score

74. Are the Workload Security Capabilities requirements complete?

<--- Score

75. Is there a Workload Security Capabilities management charter, including stakeholder case, problem and goal statements, scope, milestones, roles and responsibilities, communication plan?

<--- Score

76. Why are you doing Workload Security Capabilities and what is the scope?

<--- Score

77. Has the Workload Security Capabilities work been fairly and/or equitably divided and delegated among team members who are qualified and capable to perform the work? Has everyone contributed?

<--- Score

78. Is Workload Security Capabilities currently on schedule according to the plan?
<--- Score

79. Are all requirements met?
<--- Score

80. What is out-of-scope initially?
<--- Score

81. What baselines are required to be defined and managed?
<--- Score

82. What are the dynamics of the communication plan?
<--- Score

83. What constraints exist that might impact the team?
<--- Score

84. How do you keep key subject matter experts in the loop?
<--- Score

85. How will variation in the actual durations of each activity be dealt with to ensure that the expected Workload Security Capabilities results are met?
<--- Score

86. How do you manage unclear Workload Security Capabilities requirements?
<--- Score

87. Are resources adequate for the scope?

<--- Score

88. How have you defined all Workload Security Capabilities requirements first?
<--- Score

89. What are the Roles and Responsibilities for each team member and its leadership? Where is this documented?
<--- Score

90. Have the customer needs been translated into specific, measurable requirements? How?
<--- Score

91. What are the Workload Security Capabilities use cases?
<--- Score

92. What are the boundaries of the scope? What is in bounds and what is not? What is the start point? What is the stop point?
<--- Score

93. How would you define the culture at your organization, how susceptible is it to Workload Security Capabilities changes?
<--- Score

94. What are the rough order estimates on cost savings/opportunities that Workload Security Capabilities brings?
<--- Score

95. How are consistent Workload Security Capabilities definitions important?

<--- Score

96. Are different versions of process maps needed to account for the different types of inputs?
<--- Score

97. Is the Workload Security Capabilities scope manageable?
<--- Score

98. What customer feedback methods were used to solicit their input?
<--- Score

99. How can the value of Workload Security Capabilities be defined?
<--- Score

100. Is there a completed, verified, and validated high-level 'as is' (not 'should be' or 'could be') stakeholder process map?
<--- Score

101. The political context: who holds power?
<--- Score

102. Is the improvement team aware of the different versions of a process: what they think it is vs. what it actually is vs. what it should be vs. what it could be?
<--- Score

103. Who defines (or who defined) the rules and roles?
<--- Score

104. When is/was the Workload Security Capabilities start date?

<--- Score

105. What are the tasks and definitions?
<--- Score

106. Are approval levels defined for contracts and supplements to contracts?
<--- Score

107. How do you gather the stories?
<--- Score

108. What defines best in class?
<--- Score

109. What are the requirements for audit information?
<--- Score

110. Are task requirements clearly defined?
<--- Score

111. Do you have organizational privacy requirements?
<--- Score

112. How did the Workload Security Capabilities manager receive input to the development of a Workload Security Capabilities improvement plan and the estimated completion dates/times of each activity?
<--- Score

113. Has a team charter been developed and communicated?
<--- Score

114. Has a project plan, Gantt chart, or similar been developed/completed?
<--- Score

115. Are there different segments of customers?
<--- Score

116. Have all basic functions of Workload Security Capabilities been defined?
<--- Score

117. What key stakeholder process output measure(s) does Workload Security Capabilities leverage and how?
<--- Score

118. Have specific policy objectives been defined?
<--- Score

119. Are accountability and ownership for Workload Security Capabilities clearly defined?
<--- Score

120. What are the compelling stakeholder reasons for embarking on Workload Security Capabilities?
<--- Score

121. How is the team tracking and documenting its work?
<--- Score

122. How does the Workload Security Capabilities manager ensure against scope creep?
<--- Score

123. Has a Workload Security Capabilities

requirement not been met?
<--- Score

124. Is Workload Security Capabilities required?
<--- Score

125. Is there regularly 100% attendance at the team meetings? If not, have appointed substitutes attended to preserve cross-functionality and full representation?
<--- Score

126. What is the scope of the Workload Security Capabilities effort?
<--- Score

127. Do you have a Workload Security Capabilities success story or case study ready to tell and share?
<--- Score

128. What knowledge or experience is required?
<--- Score

129. What critical content must be communicated – who, what, when, where, and how?
<--- Score

130. What is the context?
<--- Score

131. What system do you use for gathering Workload Security Capabilities information?
<--- Score

132. Are required metrics defined, what are they?
<--- Score

133. Who are the Workload Security Capabilities improvement team members, including Management Leads and Coaches?
<--- Score

134. Have all of the relationships been defined properly?
<--- Score

135. Is Workload Security Capabilities linked to key stakeholder goals and objectives?
<--- Score

Add up total points for this section:
_____ = Total points for this section

Divided by: _____ (number of statements answered) = _____
Average score for this section

Transfer your score to the Workload Security Capabilities Index at the beginning of the Self-Assessment.

CRITERION #3: MEASURE:

1. Among the Workload Security Capabilities product and service cost to be estimated, which is considered hardest to estimate?
<--- Score

2. Are there any easy-to-implement alternatives to Workload Security Capabilities? Sometimes other solutions are available that do not require the cost implications of a full-blown project?

<--- Score

3. Where is it measured?
<--- Score

4. How do you aggregate measures across priorities?
<--- Score

5. When should you bother with diagrams?
<--- Score

6. Have design-to-cost goals been established?
<--- Score

7. How will you measure your Workload Security Capabilities effectiveness?
<--- Score

8. What do you measure and why?
<--- Score

9. What measurements are being captured?
<--- Score

10. What are hidden Workload Security Capabilities quality costs?
<--- Score

11. How do you verify and develop ideas and innovations?
<--- Score

12. What causes extra work or rework?
<--- Score

13. When are costs are incurred?
<--- Score

14. What causes mismanagement?
<--- Score

15. What causes investor action?
<--- Score

16. How much does it cost?
<--- Score

17. How sensitive must the Workload Security Capabilities strategy be to cost?
<--- Score

18. What is the cost of rework?
<--- Score

19. What could cause you to change course?
<--- Score

20. How do you verify and validate the Workload Security Capabilities data?
<--- Score

21. What is an unallowable cost?
<--- Score

22. How frequently do you track Workload Security Capabilities measures?
<--- Score

23. Is the solution cost-effective?
<--- Score

24. What could cause delays in the schedule?
<--- Score

25. What disadvantage does this cause for the user?
<--- Score

26. Are you aware of what could cause a problem?
<--- Score

27. How do your measurements capture actionable Workload Security Capabilities information for use in exceeding your customers expectations and securing your customers engagement?
<--- Score

28. What are your primary costs, revenues, assets?
<--- Score

29. Are the measurements objective?
<--- Score

30. How are costs allocated?
<--- Score

31. Was a business case (cost/benefit) developed?
<--- Score

32. What are your customers expectations and measures?
<--- Score

33. Does a Workload Security Capabilities quantification method exist?
<--- Score

34. What does your operating model cost?

<--- Score

35. How can you manage cost down?
<--- Score

36. How is the value delivered by Workload Security Capabilities being measured?
<--- Score

37. What can be used to verify compliance?
<--- Score

38. Did you tackle the cause or the symptom?
<--- Score

39. What happens if cost savings do not materialize?
<--- Score

40. What is measured? Why?
<--- Score

41. Which measures and indicators matter?
<--- Score

42. Do you effectively measure and reward individual and team performance?
<--- Score

43. How can you reduce costs?
<--- Score

44. Is the cost worth the Workload Security Capabilities effort ?
<--- Score

45. Where is the cost?
<--- Score

46. What are the Workload Security Capabilities investment costs?
<--- Score

47. How do you measure variability?
<--- Score

48. Do you have an issue in getting priority?
<--- Score

49. How will effects be measured?
<--- Score

50. What users will be impacted?
<--- Score

51. What are the strategic priorities for this year?
<--- Score

52. How will success or failure be measured?
<--- Score

53. What relevant entities could be measured?
<--- Score

54. What is the root cause(s) of the problem?
<--- Score

55. Have you included everything in your Workload Security Capabilities cost models?
<--- Score

56. Which Workload Security Capabilities impacts are

significant?
<--- Score

57. How do you verify performance?
<--- Score

58. How is progress measured?
<--- Score

59. How do you verify the authenticity of the data and information used?
<--- Score

60. How do you measure success?
<--- Score

61. How do you control the overall costs of your work processes?
<--- Score

62. What is the total cost related to deploying Workload Security Capabilities, including any consulting or professional services?
<--- Score

63. What are allowable costs?
<--- Score

64. What would it cost to replace your technology?
<--- Score

65. Are the units of measure consistent?
<--- Score

66. Is it possible to estimate the impact of unanticipated complexity such as wrong or failed

assumptions, feedback, etcetera on proposed reforms?
<--- Score

67. What are the costs of reform?
<--- Score

68. How will costs be allocated?
<--- Score

69. How long to keep data and how to manage retention costs?
<--- Score

70. What are your key Workload Security Capabilities organizational performance measures, including key short and longer-term financial measures?
<--- Score

71. What measurements are possible, practicable and meaningful?
<--- Score

72. What are the costs?
<--- Score

73. How do you verify your resources?
<--- Score

74. How are measurements made?
<--- Score

75. Which costs should be taken into account?
<--- Score

76. Is there an opportunity to verify requirements?

<--- Score

77. Are supply costs steady or fluctuating?
<--- Score

78. Do you have any cost Workload Security
Capabilities limitation requirements?
<--- Score

79. What are the uncertainties surrounding estimates
of impact?
<--- Score

80. How do you prevent mis-estimating cost?
<--- Score

81. What evidence is there and what is measured?
<--- Score

82. What is the cause of any Workload Security
Capabilities gaps?
<--- Score

83. How do you verify if Workload Security Capabilities
is built right?
<--- Score

84. What drives O&M cost?
<--- Score

85. What are your operating costs?
<--- Score

86. What would be a real cause for concern?
<--- Score

87. How do you verify the Workload Security Capabilities requirements quality?

<--- Score

88. Are there competing Workload Security Capabilities priorities?

<--- Score

89. Do you aggressively reward and promote the people who have the biggest impact on creating excellent Workload Security Capabilities services/ products?

<--- Score

90. What methods are feasible and acceptable to estimate the impact of reforms?

<--- Score

91. What do people want to verify?

<--- Score

92. Are you able to realize any cost savings?

<--- Score

93. Are the Workload Security Capabilities benefits worth its costs?

<--- Score

94. What are the costs of delaying Workload Security Capabilities action?

<--- Score

95. What is your decision requirements diagram?

<--- Score

96. Has a cost center been established?

<--- Score

97. How is performance measured?
<--- Score

98. When a disaster occurs, who gets priority?
<--- Score

99. Why do you expend time and effort to implement measurement, for whom?
<--- Score

100. How can you measure Workload Security Capabilities in a systematic way?
<--- Score

101. What are the estimated costs of proposed changes?
<--- Score

102. Are missed Workload Security Capabilities opportunities costing your organization money?
<--- Score

103. What are the types and number of measures to use?
<--- Score

104. What details are required of the Workload Security Capabilities cost structure?
<--- Score

105. Are Workload Security Capabilities vulnerabilities categorized and prioritized?
<--- Score

106. At what cost?
<--- Score

107. What harm might be caused?
<--- Score

108. How will your organization measure success?
<--- Score

109. Are indirect costs charged to the Workload Security Capabilities program?
<--- Score

110. What causes innovation to fail or succeed in your organization?
<--- Score

111. Have you made assumptions about the shape of the future, particularly its impact on your customers and competitors?
<--- Score

112. Does the Workload Security Capabilities task fit the client's priorities?
<--- Score

113. How will measures be used to manage and adapt?
<--- Score

114. Who should receive measurement reports?
<--- Score

115. What are the Workload Security Capabilities key cost drivers?
<--- Score

116. What is your Workload Security Capabilities quality cost segregation study?
<--- Score

117. Who pays the cost?
<--- Score

118. Will Workload Security Capabilities have an impact on current business continuity, disaster recovery processes and/or infrastructure?
<--- Score

119. What are the current costs of the Workload Security Capabilities process?
<--- Score

120. What does losing customers cost your organization?
<--- Score

121. Do you have a flow diagram of what happens?
<--- Score

122. Are you taking your company in the direction of better and revenue or cheaper and cost?
<--- Score

123. What are the operational costs after Workload Security Capabilities deployment?
<--- Score

124. How to cause the change?
<--- Score

125. What is the total fixed cost?

<--- Score

126. What potential environmental factors impact the Workload Security Capabilities effort?
<--- Score

127. How do you quantify and qualify impacts?
<--- Score

128. What does a Test Case verify?
<--- Score

129. How do you measure lifecycle phases?
<--- Score

130. What are the costs and benefits?
<--- Score

131. Why do the measurements/indicators matter?
<--- Score

132. How will you measure success?
<--- Score

Add up total points for this section:
_ _ _ _ _ = Total points for this section

Divided by: _ _ _ _ _ _ (number of statements answered) = _ _ _ _ _ _
Average score for this section

Transfer your score to the Workload Security Capabilities Index at the beginning of the Self-Assessment.

CRITERION #4: ANALYZE:

INTENT: Analyze causes, assumptions and hypotheses.

In my belief, the answer to this question is clearly defined:

5 Strongly Agree

4 Agree

3 Neutral

2 Disagree

1 Strongly Disagree

1. Were Pareto charts (or similar) used to portray the 'heavy hitters' (or key sources of variation)?
<--- Score

2. Was a detailed process map created to amplify critical steps of the 'as is' stakeholder process?
<--- Score

3. How do your work systems and key work processes relate to and capitalize on your core competencies?

<--- Score

4. Is the suppliers process defined and controlled?
<--- Score

5. Who is involved with workflow mapping?
<--- Score

6. What are your Workload Security Capabilities processes?
<--- Score

7. How is the data gathered?
<--- Score

8. What information qualified as important?
<--- Score

9. What does the data say about the performance of the stakeholder process?
<--- Score

10. What are the personnel training and qualifications required?
<--- Score

11. Do your leaders quickly bounce back from setbacks?
<--- Score

12. What are your current levels and trends in key Workload Security Capabilities measures or indicators of product and process performance that are important to and directly serve your customers?
<--- Score

13. Has an output goal been set?
<--- Score

14. How is the Workload Security Capabilities Value Stream Mapping managed?
<--- Score

15. What are your current levels and trends in key measures or indicators of Workload Security Capabilities product and process performance that are important to and directly serve your customers? How do these results compare with the performance of your competitors and other organizations with similar offerings?
<--- Score

16. What process should you select for improvement?
<--- Score

17. What is the Workload Security Capabilities Driver?
<--- Score

18. How do you ensure that the Workload Security Capabilities opportunity is realistic?
<--- Score

19. What are evaluation criteria for the output?
<--- Score

20. Is there a strict change management process?
<--- Score

21. Is there an established change management process?
<--- Score

22. How is the way you as the leader think and process information affecting your organizational culture?
<--- Score

23. How is Workload Security Capabilities data gathered?
<--- Score

24. How was the detailed process map generated, verified, and validated?
<--- Score

25. What tools were used to narrow the list of possible causes?
<--- Score

26. What are the processes for audit reporting and management?
<--- Score

27. Have the problem and goal statements been updated to reflect the additional knowledge gained from the analyze phase?
<--- Score

28. How will corresponding data be collected?
<--- Score

29. Were any designed experiments used to generate additional insight into the data analysis?
<--- Score

30. What other jobs or tasks affect the performance of the steps in the Workload Security Capabilities process?
<--- Score

31. Is there any way to speed up the process?
<--- Score

32. How do you define collaboration and team output?
<--- Score

33. What qualifications are needed?
<--- Score

34. Do your contracts/agreements contain data security obligations?
<--- Score

35. Is the final output clearly identified?
<--- Score

36. What are the necessary qualifications?
<--- Score

37. An organizationally feasible system request is one that considers the mission, goals and objectives of the organization, key questions are: is the Workload Security Capabilities solution request practical and will it solve a problem or take advantage of an opportunity to achieve company goals?
<--- Score

38. How does the organization define, manage, and improve its Workload Security Capabilities processes?
<--- Score

39. What is the cost of poor quality as supported by the team's analysis?

<--- Score

40. Record-keeping requirements flow from the records needed as inputs, outputs, controls and for transformation of a Workload Security Capabilities process, are the records needed as inputs to the Workload Security Capabilities process available?
<--- Score

41. What Workload Security Capabilities data will be collected?
<--- Score

42. What data is gathered?
<--- Score

43. What internal processes need improvement?
<--- Score

44. What Workload Security Capabilities data should be managed?
<--- Score

45. What qualifies as competition?
<--- Score

46. What are the Workload Security Capabilities design outputs?
<--- Score

47. How many input/output points does it require?
<--- Score

48. Where can you get qualified talent today?
<--- Score

49. How do you use Workload Security Capabilities data and information to support organizational decision making and innovation?
<--- Score

50. Has data output been validated?
<--- Score

51. What Workload Security Capabilities data should be collected?
<--- Score

52. What are your outputs?
<--- Score

53. How will the data be checked for quality?
<--- Score

54. What is the complexity of the output produced?
<--- Score

55. Who will gather what data?
<--- Score

56. Are all team members qualified for all tasks?
<--- Score

57. Do quality systems drive continuous improvement?
<--- Score

58. What other organizational variables, such as reward systems or communication systems, affect the performance of this Workload Security Capabilities process?

<--- Score

59. What types of data do your Workload Security Capabilities indicators require?
<--- Score

60. How will the change process be managed?
<--- Score

61. What qualifications and skills do you need?
<--- Score

62. What is your organizations system for selecting qualified vendors?
<--- Score

63. What is the output?
<--- Score

64. Are all staff in core Workload Security Capabilities subjects Highly Qualified?
<--- Score

65. When should a process be art not science?
<--- Score

66. What training and qualifications will you need?
<--- Score

67. Is pre-qualification of suppliers carried out?
<--- Score

68. What were the financial benefits resulting from any 'ground fruit or low-hanging fruit' (quick fixes)?
<--- Score

69. What successful thing are you doing today that may be blinding you to new growth opportunities?
<--- Score

70. What are the best opportunities for value improvement?
<--- Score

71. What quality tools were used to get through the analyze phase?
<--- Score

72. Is the required Workload Security Capabilities data gathered?
<--- Score

73. How has the Workload Security Capabilities data been gathered?
<--- Score

74. Are your outputs consistent?
<--- Score

75. Who owns what data?
<--- Score

76. What, related to, Workload Security Capabilities processes does your organization outsource?
<--- Score

77. Do you understand your management processes today?
<--- Score

78. Have you defined which data is gathered how?
<--- Score

79. How difficult is it to qualify what Workload Security Capabilities ROI is?
<--- Score

80. How do you promote understanding that opportunity for improvement is not criticism of the status quo, or the people who created the status quo?
<--- Score

81. Is data and process analysis, root cause analysis and quantifying the gap/opportunity in place?
<--- Score

82. Are Workload Security Capabilities changes recognized early enough to be approved through the regular process?
<--- Score

83. What do you need to qualify?
<--- Score

84. Should you invest in industry-recognized qualifications?
<--- Score

85. What conclusions were drawn from the team's data collection and analysis? How did the team reach these conclusions?
<--- Score

86. Which Workload Security Capabilities data should be retained?
<--- Score

87. What qualifications do Workload Security Capabilities leaders need?
<--- Score

88. What did the team gain from developing a sub-process map?
<--- Score

89. How do you implement and manage your work processes to ensure that they meet design requirements?
<--- Score

90. What are the Workload Security Capabilities business drivers?
<--- Score

91. Identify an operational issue in your organization, for example, could a particular task be done more quickly or more efficiently by Workload Security Capabilities?
<--- Score

92. Can you add value to the current Workload Security Capabilities decision-making process (largely qualitative) by incorporating uncertainty modeling (more quantitative)?
<--- Score

93. What resources go in to get the desired output?
<--- Score

94. How often will data be collected for measures?
<--- Score

95. What Workload Security Capabilities metrics are

outputs of the process?
<--- Score

96. Do your employees have the opportunity to do what they do best everyday?
<--- Score

97. Where is the data coming from to measure compliance?
<--- Score

98. Do you, as a leader, bounce back quickly from setbacks?
<--- Score

99. What are your best practices for minimizing Workload Security Capabilities project risk, while demonstrating incremental value and quick wins throughout the Workload Security Capabilities project lifecycle?
<--- Score

100. Were there any improvement opportunities identified from the process analysis?
<--- Score

101. Who gets your output?
<--- Score

102. Was a cause-and-effect diagram used to explore the different types of causes (or sources of variation)?
<--- Score

103. Do staff qualifications match your project?
<--- Score

104. Where is Workload Security Capabilities data gathered?

<--- Score

105. Is the gap/opportunity displayed and communicated in financial terms?

<--- Score

106. Who qualifies to gain access to data?

<--- Score

107. Is the Workload Security Capabilities process severely broken such that a re-design is necessary?

<--- Score

108. Who will facilitate the team and process?

<--- Score

109. What were the crucial 'moments of truth' on the process map?

<--- Score

110. Is the performance gap determined?

<--- Score

111. What process improvements will be needed?

<--- Score

112. What are your key performance measures or indicators and in-process measures for the control and improvement of your Workload Security Capabilities processes?

<--- Score

113. What methods do you use to gather Workload Security Capabilities data?

<--- Score

114. What qualifications are necessary?
<--- Score

115. How can risk management be tied procedurally to process elements?
<--- Score

116. How are outputs preserved and protected?
<--- Score

117. What kind of crime could a potential new hire have committed that would not only not disqualify him/her from being hired by your organization, but would actually indicate that he/she might be a particularly good fit?
<--- Score

118. How do you identify specific Workload Security Capabilities investment opportunities and emerging trends?
<--- Score

119. What are the disruptive Workload Security Capabilities technologies that enable your organization to radically change your business processes?
<--- Score

120. Who is involved in the management review process?
<--- Score

121. How much data can be collected in the given timeframe?

<--- Score

122. What is your organizations process which leads to recognition of value generation?
<--- Score

123. Think about the functions involved in your Workload Security Capabilities project, what processes flow from these functions?
<--- Score

124. Do you have the authority to produce the output?
<--- Score

125. What tools were used to generate the list of possible causes?
<--- Score

126. What will drive Workload Security Capabilities change?
<--- Score

127. What is the oversight process?
<--- Score

128. What are the revised rough estimates of the financial savings/opportunity for Workload Security Capabilities improvements?
<--- Score

129. What data do you need to collect?
<--- Score

130. Think about some of the processes you undertake within your organization, which do you

own?

<--- Score

131. What systems/processes must you excel at?

<--- Score

132. What controls do you have in place to protect data?

<--- Score

Add up total points for this section:

_ _ _ _ _ = Total points for this section

Divided by: _ _ _ _ _ _ (number of
statements answered) = _ _ _ _ _ _
Average score for this section

Transfer your score to the Workload
Security Capabilities Index at the
beginning of the Self-Assessment.

CRITERION #5: IMPROVE:

INTENT: Develop a practical solution.
Innovate, establish and test the
solution and to measure the results.

In my belief, the answer to this
question is clearly defined:

5 Strongly Agree

4 Agree

3 Neutral

2 Disagree

1 Strongly Disagree

1. What risks do you need to manage?
<--- Score

2. What are the expected Workload Security
Capabilities results?
<--- Score

3. How will you measure the results?
<--- Score

4. What tools were used to evaluate the potential solutions?
<--- Score

5. Is a solution implementation plan established, including schedule/work breakdown structure, resources, risk management plan, cost/budget, and control plan?
<--- Score

6. How do you improve productivity?
<--- Score

7. Who do you report Workload Security Capabilities results to?
<--- Score

8. How does the team improve its work?
<--- Score

9. What lessons, if any, from a pilot were incorporated into the design of the full-scale solution?
<--- Score

10. Who are the key stakeholders for the Workload Security Capabilities evaluation?
<--- Score

11. What criteria will you use to assess your Workload Security Capabilities risks?
<--- Score

12. How will you know that a change is an improvement?
<--- Score

13. Have you achieved Workload Security Capabilities improvements?
<--- Score

14. Explorations of the frontiers of Workload Security Capabilities will help you build influence, improve Workload Security Capabilities, optimize decision making, and sustain change, what is your approach?
<--- Score

15. Is Workload Security Capabilities documentation maintained?
<--- Score

16. Why improve in the first place?
<--- Score

17. What communications are necessary to support the implementation of the solution?
<--- Score

18. Who manages supplier risk management in your organization?
<--- Score

19. What improvements have been achieved?
<--- Score

20. What are the Workload Security Capabilities security risks?
<--- Score

21. What error proofing will be done to address some of the discrepancies observed in the 'as is' process?

<--- Score

22. How do you go about comparing Workload Security Capabilities approaches/solutions?
<--- Score

23. Is there a small-scale pilot for proposed improvement(s)? What conclusions were drawn from the outcomes of a pilot?
<--- Score

24. If you could go back in time five years, what decision would you make differently? What is your best guess as to what decision you're making today you might regret five years from now?
<--- Score

25. Is the Workload Security Capabilities solution sustainable?
<--- Score

26. Which of the recognised risks out of all risks can be most likely transferred?
<--- Score

27. What should a proof of concept or pilot accomplish?
<--- Score

28. Is a contingency plan established?
<--- Score

29. Are risk management tasks balanced centrally and locally?
<--- Score

30. Is pilot data collected and analyzed?
<--- Score

31. What actually has to improve and by how much?
<--- Score

32. What area needs the greatest improvement?
<--- Score

33. For estimation problems, how do you develop an estimation statement?
<--- Score

34. Who should make the Workload Security Capabilities decisions?
<--- Score

35. What tools do you use once you have decided on a Workload Security Capabilities strategy and more importantly how do you choose?
<--- Score

36. Is the implementation plan designed?
<--- Score

37. Is the Workload Security Capabilities documentation thorough?
<--- Score

38. How can the phases of Workload Security Capabilities development be identified?
<--- Score

39. How do you define the solutions' scope?
<--- Score

40. Are events managed to resolution?
<--- Score

41. Does a good decision guarantee a good outcome?
<--- Score

42. What strategies for Workload Security Capabilities improvement are successful?
<--- Score

43. How do you manage and improve your Workload Security Capabilities work systems to deliver customer value and achieve organizational success and sustainability?
<--- Score

44. What is the Workload Security Capabilities's sustainability risk?
<--- Score

45. Who do you report Workload Security Capabilities results to?
<--- Score

46. In the past few months, what is the smallest change you have made that has had the biggest positive result? What was it about that small change that produced the large return?
<--- Score

47. Risk factors: what are the characteristics of Workload Security Capabilities that make it risky?
<--- Score

48. Are procedures documented for managing Workload Security Capabilities risks?

<--- Score

49. Who will be responsible for making the decisions to include or exclude requested changes once Workload Security Capabilities is underway?
<--- Score

50. What tools were used to tap into the creativity and encourage 'outside the box' thinking?
<--- Score

51. Who are the Workload Security Capabilities decision-makers?
<--- Score

52. What do you want to improve?
<--- Score

53. How are Workload Security Capabilities risks managed?
<--- Score

54. Which Workload Security Capabilities solution is appropriate?
<--- Score

55. How do you measure risk?
<--- Score

56. Do you combine technical expertise with business knowledge and Workload Security Capabilities Key topics include lifecycles, development approaches, requirements and how to make a business case?
<--- Score

57. What is Workload Security Capabilities risk?

<--- Score

58. Does the goal represent a desired result that can be measured?
<--- Score

59. Can you integrate quality management and risk management?
<--- Score

60. For decision problems, how do you develop a decision statement?
<--- Score

61. Is there any other Workload Security Capabilities solution?
<--- Score

62. Is there a high likelihood that any recommendations will achieve their intended results?
<--- Score

63. How do you deal with Workload Security Capabilities risk?
<--- Score

64. Is there a cost/benefit analysis of optimal solution(s)?
<--- Score

65. Will the controls trigger any other risks?
<--- Score

66. Was a Workload Security Capabilities charter developed?
<--- Score

67. Who controls the risk?
<--- Score

68. What are the implications of the one critical Workload Security Capabilities decision 10 minutes, 10 months, and 10 years from now?
<--- Score

69. At what point will vulnerability assessments be performed once Workload Security Capabilities is put into production (e.g., ongoing Risk Management after implementation)?
<--- Score

70. How will you know that you have improved?
<--- Score

71. Who will be using the results of the measurement activities?
<--- Score

72. How do you keep improving Workload Security Capabilities?
<--- Score

73. Who will be responsible for documenting the Workload Security Capabilities requirements in detail?
<--- Score

74. What attendant changes will need to be made to ensure that the solution is successful?
<--- Score

75. Was a pilot designed for the proposed solution(s)?
<--- Score

76. Is supporting Workload Security Capabilities documentation required?

<--- Score

77. What is the implementation plan?

<--- Score

78. What were the criteria for evaluating a Workload Security Capabilities pilot?

<--- Score

79. Have you identified breakpoints and/or risk tolerances that will trigger broad consideration of a potential need for intervention or modification of strategy?

<--- Score

80. Would you develop a Workload Security Capabilities Communication Strategy?

<--- Score

81. Is the solution technically practical?

<--- Score

82. Who makes the Workload Security Capabilities decisions in your organization?

<--- Score

83. Is any Workload Security Capabilities documentation required?

<--- Score

84. What is Workload Security Capabilities's impact on utilizing the best solution(s)?

<--- Score

85. To what extent does management recognize Workload Security Capabilities as a tool to increase the results?
<--- Score

86. What to do with the results or outcomes of measurements?
<--- Score

87. Is risk periodically assessed?
<--- Score

88. Who manages Workload Security Capabilities risk?
<--- Score

89. What does the 'should be' process map/design look like?
<--- Score

90. When you map the key players in your own work and the types/domains of relationships with them, which relationships do you find easy and which challenging, and why?
<--- Score

91. How can you improve performance?
<--- Score

92. Can you identify any significant risks or exposures to Workload Security Capabilities third- parties (vendors, service providers, alliance partners etc) that concern you?
<--- Score

93. What resources are required for the improvement

efforts?
<--- Score

94. How do the Workload Security Capabilities results compare with the performance of your competitors and other organizations with similar offerings?
<--- Score

95. How risky is your organization?
<--- Score

96. Risk events: what are the things that could go wrong?
<--- Score

97. Are decisions made in a timely manner?
<--- Score

98. Is the optimal solution selected based on testing and analysis?
<--- Score

99. How do you measure progress and evaluate training effectiveness?
<--- Score

100. How can skill-level changes improve Workload Security Capabilities?
<--- Score

101. Is the scope clearly documented?
<--- Score

102. What tools were most useful during the improve phase?
<--- Score

103. What alternative responses are available to manage risk?

<--- Score

104. Do you cover the five essential competencies: Communication, Collaboration,Innovation, Adaptability, and Leadership that improve an organizations ability to leverage the new Workload Security Capabilities in a volatile global economy?

<--- Score

105. How does your organization evaluate strategic Workload Security Capabilities success?

<--- Score

106. Are risk triggers captured?

<--- Score

107. What can you do to improve?

<--- Score

108. What practices helps your organization to develop its capacity to recognize patterns?

<--- Score

109. Who are the people involved in developing and implementing Workload Security Capabilities?

<--- Score

110. How can you better manage risk?

<--- Score

111. How do you decide how much to remunerate an employee?

<--- Score

112. How do you improve Workload Security Capabilities service perception, and satisfaction?
<--- Score

113. Can the solution be designed and implemented within an acceptable time period?
<--- Score

114. Do you need to do a usability evaluation?
<--- Score

115. How do you link measurement and risk?
<--- Score

116. How do you mitigate Workload Security Capabilities risk?
<--- Score

117. Who controls key decisions that will be made?
<--- Score

118. What is the team's contingency plan for potential problems occurring in implementation?
<--- Score

119. Risk Identification: What are the possible risk events your organization faces in relation to Workload Security Capabilities?
<--- Score

120. What went well, what should change, what can improve?
<--- Score

121. How significant is the improvement in the eyes of the end user?
<--- Score

122. How will you recognize and celebrate results?
<--- Score

123. Is the measure of success for Workload Security Capabilities understandable to a variety of people?
<--- Score

124. Workload Security Capabilities risk decisions: whose call Is It?
<--- Score

125. How do you measure improved Workload Security Capabilities service perception, and satisfaction?
<--- Score

126. Were any criteria developed to assist the team in testing and evaluating potential solutions?
<--- Score

127. What is the risk?
<--- Score

128. How do you improve your likelihood of success ?
<--- Score

129. Are the most efficient solutions problem-specific?
<--- Score

130. What are the affordable Workload Security Capabilities risks?

<--- Score

131. What are your current levels and trends in key measures or indicators of workforce and leader development?
<--- Score

132. What were the underlying assumptions on the cost-benefit analysis?
<--- Score

133. What needs improvement? Why?
<--- Score

134. How is knowledge sharing about risk management improved?
<--- Score

135. Do vendor agreements bring new compliance risk ?
<--- Score

136. Where do the Workload Security Capabilities decisions reside?
<--- Score

137. How are policy decisions made and where?
<--- Score

138. Do those selected for the Workload Security Capabilities team have a good general understanding of what Workload Security Capabilities is all about?
<--- Score

Add up total points for this section:

_____ = Total points for this section

Divided by: _____ (number of
statements answered) = _____
Average score for this section

Transfer your score to the Workload
Security Capabilities Index at the
beginning of the Self-Assessment.

CRITERION #6: CONTROL:

INTENT: Implement the practical solution. Maintain the performance and correct possible complications.

In my belief, the answer to this question is clearly defined:

5 Strongly Agree

4 Agree

3 Neutral

2 Disagree

1 Strongly Disagree

1. Are you measuring, monitoring and predicting Workload Security Capabilities activities to optimize operations and profitability, and enhancing outcomes?
<--- Score

2. Are the planned controls in place?
<--- Score

3. How will the process owner and team be able to hold the gains?
<--- Score

4. Is a response plan in place for when the input, process, or output measures indicate an 'out-of-control' condition?
<--- Score

5. What are your results for key measures or indicators of the accomplishment of your Workload Security Capabilities strategy and action plans, including building and strengthening core competencies?
<--- Score

6. Can support from partners be adjusted?
<--- Score

7. How will the process owner verify improvement in present and future sigma levels, process capabilities?
<--- Score

8. What are the key elements of your Workload Security Capabilities performance improvement system, including your evaluation, organizational learning, and innovation processes?
<--- Score

9. What other systems, operations, processes, and infrastructures (hiring practices, staffing, training, incentives/rewards, metrics/dashboards/scorecards, etc.) need updates, additions, changes, or deletions in order to facilitate knowledge transfer and improvements?
<--- Score

10. What is the control/monitoring plan?
<--- Score

11. How will you measure your QA plan's effectiveness?
<--- Score

12. Who will be in control?
<--- Score

13. What do you measure to verify effectiveness gains?
<--- Score

14. What is the best design framework for Workload Security Capabilities organization now that, in a post industrial-age if the top-down, command and control model is no longer relevant?
<--- Score

15. What are you attempting to measure/monitor?
<--- Score

16. How will new or emerging customer needs/ requirements be checked/communicated to orient the process toward meeting the new specifications and continually reducing variation?
<--- Score

17. Is there a control plan in place for sustaining improvements (short and long-term)?
<--- Score

18. What other areas of the group might benefit from the Workload Security Capabilities team's

improvements, knowledge, and learning?
<--- Score

19. Has the Workload Security Capabilities value of standards been quantified?
<--- Score

20. What key inputs and outputs are being measured on an ongoing basis?
<--- Score

21. How will input, process, and output variables be checked to detect for sub-optimal conditions?
<--- Score

22. In the case of a Workload Security Capabilities project, the criteria for the audit derive from implementation objectives, an audit of a Workload Security Capabilities project involves assessing whether the recommendations outlined for implementation have been met, can you track that any Workload Security Capabilities project is implemented as planned, and is it working?
<--- Score

23. How do you encourage people to take control and responsibility?
<--- Score

24. Does the Workload Security Capabilities performance meet the customer's requirements?
<--- Score

25. Who is the Workload Security Capabilities process owner?
<--- Score

26. How can you best use all of your knowledge repositories to enhance learning and sharing?
<--- Score

27. What should the next improvement project be that is related to Workload Security Capabilities?
<--- Score

28. Can you adapt and adjust to changing Workload Security Capabilities situations?
<--- Score

29. How do you establish and deploy modified action plans if circumstances require a shift in plans and rapid execution of new plans?
<--- Score

30. What adjustments to the strategies are needed?
<--- Score

31. Is the Workload Security Capabilities test/ monitoring cost justified?
<--- Score

32. You may have created your quality measures at a time when you lacked resources, technology wasn't up to the required standard, or low service levels were the industry norm. Have those circumstances changed?
<--- Score

33. Are documented procedures clear and easy to follow for the operators?
<--- Score

34. Is a response plan established and deployed?
<--- Score

35. How likely is the current Workload Security Capabilities plan to come in on schedule or on budget?
<--- Score

36. Do you monitor the Workload Security Capabilities decisions made and fine tune them as they evolve?
<--- Score

37. Will your goals reflect your program budget?
<--- Score

38. What is the standard for acceptable Workload Security Capabilities performance?
<--- Score

39. Will any special training be provided for results interpretation?
<--- Score

40. What do you stand for--and what are you against?
<--- Score

41. Are pertinent alerts monitored, analyzed and distributed to appropriate personnel?
<--- Score

42. Does job training on the documented procedures need to be part of the process team's education and training?
<--- Score

43. What do your reports reflect?

<--- Score

44. What are the performance and scale of the Workload Security Capabilities tools?
<--- Score

45. How do you plan on providing proper recognition and disclosure of supporting companies?
<--- Score

46. Is there a Workload Security Capabilities Communication plan covering who needs to get what information when?
<--- Score

47. Is there a transfer of ownership and knowledge to process owner and process team tasked with the responsibilities.
<--- Score

48. Is there an action plan in case of emergencies?
<--- Score

49. Do the viable solutions scale to future needs?
<--- Score

50. How is change control managed?
<--- Score

51. Have new or revised work instructions resulted?
<--- Score

52. Implementation Planning: is a pilot needed to test the changes before a full roll out occurs?
<--- Score

53. How might the group capture best practices and lessons learned so as to leverage improvements?
<--- Score

54. Will existing staff require re-training, for example, to learn new business processes?
<--- Score

55. Who has control over resources?
<--- Score

56. Is there a documented and implemented monitoring plan?
<--- Score

57. Does Workload Security Capabilities appropriately measure and monitor risk?
<--- Score

58. How do you select, collect, align, and integrate Workload Security Capabilities data and information for tracking daily operations and overall organizational performance, including progress relative to strategic objectives and action plans?
<--- Score

59. Will the team be available to assist members in planning investigations?
<--- Score

60. Who is going to spread your message?
<--- Score

61. What are customers monitoring?
<--- Score

62. Is there documentation that will support the successful operation of the improvement?
<--- Score

63. Who controls critical resources?
<--- Score

64. Is reporting being used or needed?
<--- Score

65. Does a troubleshooting guide exist or is it needed?
<--- Score

66. What quality tools were useful in the control phase?
<--- Score

67. Who sets the Workload Security Capabilities standards?
<--- Score

68. Are suggested corrective/restorative actions indicated on the response plan for known causes to problems that might surface?
<--- Score

69. How do controls support value?
<--- Score

70. Where do ideas that reach policy makers and planners as proposals for Workload Security Capabilities strengthening and reform actually originate?
<--- Score

71. How do senior leaders actions reflect a commitment to the organizations Workload Security Capabilities values?
<--- Score

72. Does the response plan contain a definite closed loop continual improvement scheme (e.g., plan-do-check-act)?
<--- Score

73. What are the critical parameters to watch?
<--- Score

74. Has the improved process and its steps been standardized?
<--- Score

75. How will report readings be checked to effectively monitor performance?
<--- Score

76. How do you monitor usage and cost?
<--- Score

77. Against what alternative is success being measured?
<--- Score

78. What is your plan to assess your security risks?
<--- Score

79. How will Workload Security Capabilities decisions be made and monitored?
<--- Score

80. Act/Adjust: What Do you Need to Do Differently?

<--- Score

81. Are new process steps, standards, and documentation ingrained into normal operations?
<--- Score

82. How do you plan for the cost of succession?
<--- Score

83. How is Workload Security Capabilities project cost planned, managed, monitored?
<--- Score

84. How will the day-to-day responsibilities for monitoring and continual improvement be transferred from the improvement team to the process owner?
<--- Score

85. How widespread is its use?
<--- Score

86. Is there a standardized process?
<--- Score

87. Do you monitor the effectiveness of your Workload Security Capabilities activities?
<--- Score

88. Are there documented procedures?
<--- Score

89. What can you control?
<--- Score

90. Are the planned controls working?

<--- Score

91. Is new knowledge gained imbedded in the response plan?
<--- Score

92. Are operating procedures consistent?
<--- Score

93. What is the recommended frequency of auditing?
<--- Score

94. How do you spread information?
<--- Score

95. Do the Workload Security Capabilities decisions you make today help people and the planet tomorrow?
<--- Score

96. Are the Workload Security Capabilities standards challenging?
<--- Score

97. Is there a recommended audit plan for routine surveillance inspections of Workload Security Capabilities's gains?
<--- Score

98. Is knowledge gained on process shared and institutionalized?
<--- Score

Add up total points for this section:
_ _ _ _ _ = Total points for this section

Divided by: _____ (number of
statements answered) = _____
    Average score for this section

Transfer your score to the Workload
Security Capabilities Index at the
beginning of the Self-Assessment.

CRITERION #7: SUSTAIN:

INTENT: Retain the benefits.

In my belief, the answer to this question is clearly defined:

5 Strongly Agree

4 Agree

3 Neutral

2 Disagree

1 Strongly Disagree

1. If you find that you havent accomplished one of the goals for one of the steps of the Workload Security Capabilities strategy, what will you do to fix it?
<--- Score

2. How will you insure seamless interoperability of Workload Security Capabilities moving forward?
<--- Score

3. What is it like to work for you?
<--- Score

4. Do you have the right capabilities and capacities?
<--- Score

5. If your customer were your grandmother, would you tell her to buy what you're selling?
<--- Score

6. Is Workload Security Capabilities dependent on the successful delivery of a current project?
<--- Score

7. What trophy do you want on your mantle?
<--- Score

8. How do you foster innovation?
<--- Score

9. Do you think Workload Security Capabilities accomplishes the goals you expect it to accomplish?
<--- Score

10. How do you keep records, of what?
<--- Score

11. What are strategies for increasing support and reducing opposition?
<--- Score

12. Are you making progress, and are you making progress as Workload Security Capabilities leaders?
<--- Score

13. What potential megatrends could make your business model obsolete?

<--- Score

14. Who are four people whose careers you have enhanced?
<--- Score

15. What is the overall business strategy?
<--- Score

16. How do you proactively clarify deliverables and Workload Security Capabilities quality expectations?
<--- Score

17. Would you rather sell to knowledgeable and informed customers or to uninformed customers?
<--- Score

18. What is your formula for success in Workload Security Capabilities ?
<--- Score

19. Who, on the executive team or the board, has spoken to a customer recently?
<--- Score

20. What are your personal philosophies regarding Workload Security Capabilities and how do they influence your work?
<--- Score

21. Who are the key stakeholders?
<--- Score

22. Which functions and people interact with the supplier and or customer?
<--- Score

23. Operational - will it work?
<--- Score

24. What are the short and long-term Workload Security Capabilities goals?
<--- Score

25. How do senior leaders deploy your organizations vision and values through your leadership system, to the workforce, to key suppliers and partners, and to customers and other stakeholders, as appropriate?
<--- Score

26. Do Workload Security Capabilities rules make a reasonable demand on a users capabilities?
<--- Score

27. Do you have past Workload Security Capabilities successes?
<--- Score

28. How much contingency will be available in the budget?
<--- Score

29. If you had to rebuild your organization without any traditional competitive advantages (i.e., no killer technology, promising research, innovative product/ service delivery model, etcetera), how would your people have to approach their work and collaborate together in order to create the necessary conditions for success?
<--- Score

30. Do you think you know, or do you know you

know ?
<--- Score

31. If you got fired and a new hire took your place, what would she do different?
<--- Score

32. How do you set Workload Security Capabilities stretch targets and how do you get people to not only participate in setting these stretch targets but also that they strive to achieve these?
<--- Score

33. What are the potential basics of Workload Security Capabilities fraud?
<--- Score

34. How do you accomplish your long range Workload Security Capabilities goals?
<--- Score

35. Who is responsible for Workload Security Capabilities?
<--- Score

36. What role does communication play in the success or failure of a Workload Security Capabilities project?
<--- Score

37. Which Workload Security Capabilities goals are the most important?
<--- Score

38. How can you negotiate Workload Security Capabilities successfully with a stubborn boss, an irate client, or a deceitful coworker?

<--- Score

39. Who is responsible for errors?
<--- Score

40. What is the estimated value of the project?
<--- Score

41. Is a Workload Security Capabilities breakthrough on the horizon?
<--- Score

42. At what moment would you think; Will I get fired?
<--- Score

43. Are you / should you be revolutionary or evolutionary?
<--- Score

44. Is there a work around that you can use?
<--- Score

45. What is the overall talent health of your organization as a whole at senior levels, and for each organization reporting to a member of the Senior Leadership Team?
<--- Score

46. What is the recommended frequency of auditing?
<--- Score

47. Who have you, as a company, historically been when you've been at your best?
<--- Score

48. What goals did you miss?
<--- Score

49. If no one would ever find out about your accomplishments, how would you lead differently?
<--- Score

50. What does your signature ensure?
<--- Score

51. Who is on the team?
<--- Score

52. What must you excel at?
<--- Score

53. Instead of going to current contacts for new ideas, what if you reconnected with dormant contacts-- the people you used to know? If you were going reactivate a dormant tie, who would it be?
<--- Score

54. Will there be any necessary staff changes (redundancies or new hires)?
<--- Score

55. What Workload Security Capabilities skills are most important?
<--- Score

56. What current systems have to be understood and/ or changed?
<--- Score

57. What are the essentials of internal Workload Security Capabilities management?

<--- Score

58. What is your BATNA (best alternative to a negotiated agreement)?
<--- Score

59. What is an unauthorized commitment?
<--- Score

60. How likely is it that a customer would recommend your company to a friend or colleague?
<--- Score

61. Who will be responsible for deciding whether Workload Security Capabilities goes ahead or not after the initial investigations?
<--- Score

62. What may be the consequences for the performance of an organization if all stakeholders are not consulted regarding Workload Security Capabilities?
<--- Score

63. What is the purpose of Workload Security Capabilities in relation to the mission?
<--- Score

64. What are the success criteria that will indicate that Workload Security Capabilities objectives have been met and the benefits delivered?
<--- Score

65. How do you create buy-in?
<--- Score

66. How do you know if you are successful?
<--- Score

67. How long will it take to change?
<--- Score

68. Who will provide the final approval of Workload Security Capabilities deliverables?
<--- Score

69. In retrospect, of the projects that you pulled the plug on, what percent do you wish had been allowed to keep going, and what percent do you wish had ended earlier?
<--- Score

70. How do you stay inspired?
<--- Score

71. How do you transition from the baseline to the target?
<--- Score

72. How do you go about securing Workload Security Capabilities?
<--- Score

73. If you were responsible for initiating and implementing major changes in your organization, what steps might you take to ensure acceptance of those changes?
<--- Score

74. What are the gaps in your knowledge and experience?

<--- Score

75. Whose voice (department, ethnic group, women, older workers, etc) might you have missed hearing from in your company, and how might you amplify this voice to create positive momentum for your business?
<--- Score

76. What you are going to do to affect the numbers?
<--- Score

77. How do you maintain Workload Security Capabilities's Integrity?
<--- Score

78. What trouble can you get into?
<--- Score

79. Why is Workload Security Capabilities important for you now?
<--- Score

80. What are the barriers to increased Workload Security Capabilities production?
<--- Score

81. What are internal and external Workload Security Capabilities relations?
<--- Score

82. To whom do you add value?
<--- Score

83. How can you become the company that would put you out of business?

<--- Score

84. What happens if you do not have enough funding?
<--- Score

85. Can you do all this work?
<--- Score

86. How do you ensure that implementations of Workload Security Capabilities products are done in a way that ensures safety?
<--- Score

87. What are your most important goals for the strategic Workload Security Capabilities objectives?
<--- Score

88. How do you assess the Workload Security Capabilities pitfalls that are inherent in implementing it?
<--- Score

89. Why not do Workload Security Capabilities?
<--- Score

90. If there were zero limitations, what would you do differently?
<--- Score

91. How can you become more high-tech but still be high touch?
<--- Score

92. What are the challenges?

<--- Score

93. Whom among your colleagues do you trust, and for what?
<--- Score

94. Which individuals, teams or departments will be involved in Workload Security Capabilities?
<--- Score

95. If you weren't already in this business, would you enter it today? And if not, what are you going to do about it?
<--- Score

96. Why do and why don't your customers like your organization?
<--- Score

97. What are the rules and assumptions your industry operates under? What if the opposite were true?
<--- Score

98. What are the long-term Workload Security Capabilities goals?
<--- Score

99. Do you have enough freaky customers in your portfolio pushing you to the limit day in and day out?
<--- Score

100. Is maximizing Workload Security Capabilities protection the same as minimizing Workload Security Capabilities loss?
<--- Score

101. What should you stop doing?
<--- Score

102. What is your competitive advantage?
<--- Score

103. How do you govern and fulfill your societal responsibilities?
<--- Score

104. How is implementation research currently incorporated into each of your goals?
<--- Score

105. How will you know that the Workload Security Capabilities project has been successful?
<--- Score

106. How do you deal with Workload Security Capabilities changes?
<--- Score

107. Ask yourself: how would you do this work if you only had one staff member to do it?
<--- Score

108. What Workload Security Capabilities modifications can you make work for you?
<--- Score

109. What have you done to protect your business from competitive encroachment?
<--- Score

110. Is the Workload Security Capabilities organization completing tasks effectively and efficiently?

<--- Score

111. Can the schedule be done in the given time?
<--- Score

112. Think of your Workload Security Capabilities project, what are the main functions?
<--- Score

113. Do you have an implicit bias for capital investments over people investments?
<--- Score

114. If your company went out of business tomorrow, would anyone who doesn't get a paycheck here care?
<--- Score

115. What are you trying to prove to yourself, and how might it be hijacking your life and business success?
<--- Score

116. Do you see more potential in people than they do in themselves?
<--- Score

117. When information truly is ubiquitous, when reach and connectivity are completely global, when computing resources are infinite, and when a whole new set of impossibilities are not only possible, but happening, what will that do to your business?
<--- Score

118. What could happen if you do not do it?
<--- Score

119. How will you motivate the stakeholders with the least vested interest?
<--- Score

120. How important is Workload Security Capabilities to the user organizations mission?
<--- Score

121. Will it be accepted by users?
<--- Score

122. Do you feel that more should be done in the Workload Security Capabilities area?
<--- Score

123. Is Workload Security Capabilities realistic, or are you setting yourself up for failure?
<--- Score

124. In a project to restructure Workload Security Capabilities outcomes, which stakeholders would you involve?
<--- Score

125. How are you doing compared to your industry?
<--- Score

126. What are specific Workload Security Capabilities rules to follow?
<--- Score

127. If you had to leave your organization for a year and the only communication you could have with employees/colleagues was a single paragraph, what would you write?
<--- Score

128. Who do we want your customers to become?
<--- Score

129. Are you relevant? Will you be relevant five years from now? Ten?
<--- Score

130. What is a feasible sequencing of reform initiatives over time?
<--- Score

131. What did you miss in the interview for the worst hire you ever made?
<--- Score

132. Who else should you help?
<--- Score

133. What is the craziest thing you can do?
<--- Score

134. What happens at your organization when people fail?
<--- Score

135. Marketing budgets are tighter, consumers are more skeptical, and social media has changed forever the way we talk about Workload Security Capabilities, how do you gain traction?
<--- Score

136. Do you say no to customers for no reason?
<--- Score

137. What relationships among Workload Security

Capabilities trends do you perceive?

<--- Score

138. Do you know what you are doing? And who do you call if you don't?

<--- Score

139. What will be the consequences to the stakeholder (financial, reputation etc) if Workload Security Capabilities does not go ahead or fails to deliver the objectives?

<--- Score

140. What is your Workload Security Capabilities strategy?

<--- Score

141. Are you maintaining a past–present–future perspective throughout the Workload Security Capabilities discussion?

<--- Score

142. How do you manage Workload Security Capabilities Knowledge Management (KM)?

<--- Score

143. What are the key enablers to make this Workload Security Capabilities move?

<--- Score

144. What information is critical to your organization that your executives are ignoring?

<--- Score

145. What was the last experiment you ran?

<--- Score

146. Where can you break convention?
<--- Score

147. What are the top 3 things at the forefront of your Workload Security Capabilities agendas for the next 3 years?
<--- Score

148. Why will customers want to buy your organizations products/services?
<--- Score

149. Who is the main stakeholder, with ultimate responsibility for driving Workload Security Capabilities forward?
<--- Score

150. What happens when a new employee joins the organization?
<--- Score

151. Is there any reason to believe the opposite of my current belief?
<--- Score

152. Who are your customers?
<--- Score

153. How do customers see your organization?
<--- Score

154. Are the criteria for selecting recommendations stated?
<--- Score

155. What management system can you use to leverage the Workload Security Capabilities experience, ideas, and concerns of the people closest to the work to be done?
<--- Score

156. What are current Workload Security Capabilities paradigms?
<--- Score

157. What is effective Workload Security Capabilities?
<--- Score

158. Why is it important to have senior management support for a Workload Security Capabilities project?
<--- Score

159. What are the business goals Workload Security Capabilities is aiming to achieve?
<--- Score

160. Are assumptions made in Workload Security Capabilities stated explicitly?
<--- Score

161. Do you have the right people on the bus?
<--- Score

162. What would have to be true for the option on the table to be the best possible choice?
<--- Score

163. How do you make it meaningful in connecting Workload Security Capabilities with what users do day-to-day?
<--- Score

164. Is your basic point _____ or _____?
<--- Score

165. What is the kind of project structure that would be appropriate for your Workload Security Capabilities project, should it be formal and complex, or can it be less formal and relatively simple?
<--- Score

166. What projects are going on in the organization today, and what resources are those projects using from the resource pools?
<--- Score

167. What is the range of capabilities?
<--- Score

168. How do you foster the skills, knowledge, talents, attributes, and characteristics you want to have?
<--- Score

169. What are the usability implications of Workload Security Capabilities actions?
<--- Score

170. How do you track customer value, profitability or financial return, organizational success, and sustainability?
<--- Score

171. Is there any existing Workload Security Capabilities governance structure?
<--- Score

172. What unique value proposition (UVP) do you offer?
<--- Score

173. Who do you think the world wants your organization to be?
<--- Score

174. What are you challenging?
<--- Score

175. What knowledge, skills and characteristics mark a good Workload Security Capabilities project manager?
<--- Score

176. Is your strategy driving your strategy? Or is the way in which you allocate resources driving your strategy?
<--- Score

177. Who is responsible for ensuring appropriate resources (time, people and money) are allocated to Workload Security Capabilities?
<--- Score

178. What new services of functionality will be implemented next with Workload Security Capabilities ?
<--- Score

179. Political -is anyone trying to undermine this project?
<--- Score

180. In the past year, what have you done (or could you have done) to increase the accurate perception of your company/brand as ethical and honest?
<--- Score

181. What is the funding source for this project?
<--- Score

182. What stupid rule would you most like to kill?
<--- Score

183. Is it economical; do you have the time and money?
<--- Score

184. How do you provide a safe environment -physically and emotionally?
<--- Score

185. What is the source of the strategies for Workload Security Capabilities strengthening and reform?
<--- Score

186. How will you ensure you get what you expected?
<--- Score

187. How can you incorporate support to ensure safe and effective use of Workload Security Capabilities into the services that you provide?
<--- Score

188. If you do not follow, then how to lead?
<--- Score

189. What have been your experiences in defining

long range Workload Security Capabilities goals?
<--- Score

Add up total points for this section:
_ _ _ _ _ = Total points for this section

Divided by: _ _ _ _ _ _ (number of
statements answered) = _ _ _ _ _ _
Average score for this section

Transfer your score to the Workload
Security Capabilities Index at the
beginning of the Self-Assessment.

Workload Security Capabilities and Managing Projects, Criteria for Project Managers:

1.0 Initiating Process Group: Workload Security Capabilities

1. The Workload Security Capabilities project you are managing has nine stakeholders. How many channel of communications are there between corresponding stakeholders?

2. What are the constraints?

3. Are identified risks being monitored properly, are new risks arising during the Workload Security Capabilities project or are foreseen risks occurring?

4. What is the stake of others in your Workload Security Capabilities project?

5. What are the overarching issues of your organization?

6. Just how important is your work to the overall success of the Workload Security Capabilities project?

7. Did the Workload Security Capabilities project team have the right skills?

8. Have the stakeholders identified all individual requirements pertaining to business process?

9. Does it make any difference if you am successful?

10. Do you understand all business (operational), technical, resource and vendor risks associated with the Workload Security Capabilities project?

11. Who are the Workload Security Capabilities project stakeholders?

12. Who is funding the Workload Security Capabilities project?

13. Have you evaluated the teams performance and asked for feedback?

14. What must be done?

15. How should needs be met?

16. Who supports, improves, and oversees standardized processes related to the Workload Security Capabilities projects program?

17. When are the deliverables to be generated in each phase?

18. How well defined and documented were the Workload Security Capabilities project management processes you chose to use?

19. Are you just doing busywork to pass the time?

20. What communication items need improvement?

1.1 Project Charter: Workload Security Capabilities

21. Will this replace an existing product?

22. What are the deliverables?

23. Success determination factors: how will the success of the Workload Security Capabilities project be determined from the customers perspective?

24. Major high-level milestone targets: what events measure progress?

25. Why have you chosen the aim you have set forth?

26. Why is a Workload Security Capabilities project Charter used?

27. What does it need to do?

28. Why executive support?

29. What are you striving to accomplish (measurable goal(s))?

30. What are the known stakeholder requirements?

31. When do you use a Workload Security Capabilities project Charter?

32. Who will take notes, document decisions?

33. What material?

34. Run it as as a startup?

35. What is the most common tool for helping define the detail?

36. Why do you manage integration?

37. How will you know a change is an improvement?

38. When?

39. What are the assigned resources?

40. Is it an improvement over existing products?

1.2 Stakeholder Register: Workload Security Capabilities

41. Is your organization ready for change?

42. How will reports be created?

43. How big is the gap?

44. What is the power of the stakeholder?

45. Who is managing stakeholder engagement?

46. How much influence do they have on the Workload Security Capabilities project?

47. What & Why?

48. What are the major Workload Security Capabilities project milestones requiring communications or providing communications opportunities?

49. Who are the stakeholders?

50. Who wants to talk about Security?

51. How should employers make voices heard?

52. What opportunities exist to provide communications?

1.3 Stakeholder Analysis Matrix: Workload Security Capabilities

53. Continuity, supply chain robustness?

54. What is your organizations competitors doing?

55. What resources might the stakeholder bring to the Workload Security Capabilities project?

56. Who has control over whom?

57. Effects on core activities, distraction?

58. What are innovative aspects of your organization?

59. What is the stakeholders mandate, what is mission?

60. Reputation, presence and reach?

61. How to measure the achievement of the Outputs?

62. Legislative effects?

63. Are there different rules or organizational models for men and women?

64. Management cover, succession?

65. Why do you need to manage Workload Security Capabilities project Risk?

66. Who influences whom?

67. What mechanisms are proposed to monitor and measure Workload Security Capabilities project performance in terms of social development outcomes?

68. Who determines value?

69. If you can not fix it, how do you do it differently?

70. Will the impacts be local, national or international?

71. Economy - home, abroad?

72. What do you Evaluate?

2.0 Planning Process Group: Workload Security Capabilities

73. Have operating capacities been created and/or reinforced in partners?

74. Is the schedule for the set products being met?

75. The Workload Security Capabilities project charter is created in which Workload Security Capabilities project management process group?

76. Explanation: is what the Workload Security Capabilities project intents to solve a hard question?

77. If a task is partitionable, is this a sufficient condition to reduce the Workload Security Capabilities project duration?

78. What should you do next?

79. Professionals want to know what is expected from them; what are the deliverables?

80. Is the duration of the program sufficient to ensure a cycle that will Workload Security Capabilities project the sustainability of the interventions?

81. How will you know you did it?

82. Why is it important to determine activity sequencing on Workload Security Capabilities projects?

83. Is the Workload Security Capabilities project supported by national and/or local organizations?

84. Does it make any difference if you are successful?

85. Are work methodologies, financial instruments, etc. shared among departments, organizations and Workload Security Capabilities projects?

86. Is the pace of implementing the products of the program ensuring the completeness of the results of the Workload Security Capabilities project?

87. How well did the chosen processes fit the needs of the Workload Security Capabilities project?

88. How will you do it?

89. To what extent are the visions and actions of the partners consistent or divergent with regard to the program?

90. How do you integrate Workload Security Capabilities project Planning with the Iterative/ Evolutionary SDLC?

91. Does the program have follow-up mechanisms (to verify the quality of the products, punctuality of delivery, etc.) to measure progress in the achievement of the envisaged results?

2.1 Project Management Plan: Workload Security Capabilities

92. What did not work so well?

93. Are the proposed Workload Security Capabilities project purposes different than a previously authorized Workload Security Capabilities project?

94. Are there any client staffing expectations?

95. What are the assumptions?

96. Are the existing and future without-plan conditions reasonable and appropriate?

97. Is the engineering content at a feasibility level-of-detail, and is it sufficiently complete, to provide an adequate basis for the baseline cost estimate?

98. What if, for example, the positive direction and vision of your organization causes expected trends to change resulting in greater need than expected?

99. Has the selected plan been formulated using cost effectiveness and incremental analysis techniques?

100. Why Change?

101. Is the budget realistic?

102. Will you add a schedule and diagram?

103. Are calculations and results of analyzes essentially correct?

104. What data/reports/tools/etc. do your PMs need?

105. How do you manage integration?

106. What would you do differently what did not work?

107. Who is the Workload Security Capabilities project Manager?

108. Are comparable cost estimates used for comparing, screening and selecting alternative plans, and has a reasonable cost estimate been developed for the recommended plan?

2.2 Scope Management Plan: Workload Security Capabilities

109. Are risk triggers captured?

110. Are Workload Security Capabilities project leaders committed to this Workload Security Capabilities project full time?

111. Are post milestone Workload Security Capabilities project reviews (PMPR) conducted with your organization at least once a year?

112. What are the risks that could significantly affect the scope of the Workload Security Capabilities project?

113. What are the risks that could significantly affect procuring consultant staff for the Workload Security Capabilities project?

114. Are the schedule estimates reasonable given the Workload Security Capabilities project?

115. Are meeting minutes captured and sent out after the meeting?

116. Can the Workload Security Capabilities project team do several activities in parallel?

117. Can each item be appropriately scheduled?

118. What are the risks of not having good inter-

organization cooperation on the Workload Security Capabilities project?

119. Is there a formal process for updating the Workload Security Capabilities project baseline?

120. Is each item clearly and completely defined?

121. Organizational unit (e.g., department, team, or person) who will accept responsibility for satisfactory completion of the item?

122. Have key stakeholders been identified?

123. Are all key components of a Quality Assurance Plan present?

124. What went right?

125. Is the assigned Workload Security Capabilities project manager a PMP (Certified Workload Security Capabilities project manager) and experienced?

126. Have all involved Workload Security Capabilities project stakeholders and work groups committed to the Workload Security Capabilities project?

127. What are the Quality Assurance overheads?

128. What work performance data will be captured?

2.3 Requirements Management Plan: Workload Security Capabilities

129. Is any organizational data being used or stored?

130. Could inaccurate or incomplete requirements in this Workload Security Capabilities project create a serious risk for the business?

131. Do you know which stakeholders will participate in the requirements effort?

132. Are actual resource expenditures versus planned still acceptable?

133. After the requirements are gathered and set forth on the requirements register, theyre little more than a laundry list of items. Some may be duplicates, some might conflict with others and some will be too broad or too vague to understand. Describe how the requirements will be analyzed. Who will perform the analysis?

134. Is there formal agreement on who has authority to approve a change in requirements?

135. What information regarding the Workload Security Capabilities project requirements will be reported?

136. Describe the process for rejecting the Workload Security Capabilities project requirements. Who has the authority to reject Workload Security Capabilities

project requirements?

137. Do you expect stakeholders to be cooperative?

138. Should you include sub-activities?

139. Will the contractors involved take full responsibility?

140. Did you distinguish the scope of work the contractor(s) will be required to do?

141. Will the product release be stable and mature enough to be deployed in the user community?

142. What went wrong?

143. Does the Workload Security Capabilities project have a Change Control process?

144. Is the system software (non-operating system) new to the IT Workload Security Capabilities project team?

145. Do you really need to write this document at all?

146. How detailed should the Workload Security Capabilities project get?

147. Will the Workload Security Capabilities project requirements become approved in writing?

148. Will you use an assessment of the Workload Security Capabilities project environment as a tool to discover risk to the requirements process?

2.4 Requirements Documentation: Workload Security Capabilities

149. How much testing do you need to do to prove that your system is safe?

150. Are all functions required by the customer included?

151. Verifiability. can the requirements be checked?

152. How do you get the user to tell you what they want?

153. How linear / iterative is your Requirements Gathering process (or will it be)?

154. What is a show stopper in the requirements?

155. The problem with gathering requirements is right there in the word gathering. What images does it conjure?

156. What are current process problems?

157. What kind of entity is a problem ?

158. Basic work/business process; high-level, what is being touched?

159. Does the system provide the functions which best support the customers needs?

160. Who provides requirements?

161. How to document system requirements?

162. What if the system wasn t implemented?

163. How does what is being described meet the business need?

164. What facilities must be supported by the system?

165. How does the proposed Workload Security Capabilities project contribute to the overall objectives of your organization?

166. What variations exist for a process?

167. Does your organization restrict technical alternatives?

168. Are there any requirements conflicts?

2.5 Requirements Traceability Matrix: Workload Security Capabilities

169. Will you use a Requirements Traceability Matrix?

170. How small is small enough?

171. What are the chronologies, contingencies, consequences, criteria?

172. How will it affect the stakeholders personally in career?

173. Describe the process for approving requirements so they can be added to the traceability matrix and Workload Security Capabilities project work can be performed. Will the Workload Security Capabilities project requirements become approved in writing?

174. Do you have a clear understanding of all subcontracts in place?

175. Why do you manage scope?

176. Why use a WBS?

177. What percentage of Workload Security Capabilities projects are producing traceability matrices between requirements and other work products?

178. Is there a requirements traceability process in place?

179. How do you manage scope?

180. What is the WBS?

2.6 Project Scope Statement: Workload Security Capabilities

181. If the scope changes, what will the impact be to your Workload Security Capabilities project in terms of duration, cost, quality, or any other important areas of the Workload Security Capabilities project?

182. Risks?

183. Workload Security Capabilities project lead, team lead, solution architect?

184. Did your Workload Security Capabilities project ask for this?

185. Which risks does the Workload Security Capabilities project focus on?

186. Are there adequate Workload Security Capabilities project control systems?

187. Is the plan for Workload Security Capabilities project resources adequate?

188. Will the risk plan be updated on a regular and frequent basis?

189. Will the qa related information be reported regularly as part of the status reporting mechanisms?

190. Will an issue form be in use?

191. Has the format for tracking and monitoring schedules and costs been defined?

192. Is the plan under configuration management?

193. Are there issues that could affect the existing requirements for the result, service, or product if the scope changes?

194. Is the Workload Security Capabilities project manager qualified and experienced in Workload Security Capabilities project management?

195. Why do you need to manage scope?

196. Is the scope of your Workload Security Capabilities project well defined?

197. Is the quality function identified and assigned?

198. Where and how does the team fit within your organization structure?

199. Is the Workload Security Capabilities project organization documented and on file?

200. Is this process communicated to the customer and team members?

2.7 Assumption and Constraint Log: Workload Security Capabilities

201. What strengths do you have?

202. After observing execution of process, is it in compliance with the documented Plan?

203. Diagrams and tables are included to account for complex concepts and increase overall readability?

204. Are there standards for code development?

205. Is this model reasonable?

206. Are there procedures in place to effectively manage interdependencies with other Workload Security Capabilities projects / systems?

207. Can the requirements be traced to the appropriate components of the solution, as well as test scripts?

208. Security analysis has access to information that is sanitized?

209. Is staff trained on the software technologies that are being used on the Workload Security Capabilities project?

210. Is there a Steering Committee in place?

211. Does a documented Workload Security

Capabilities project organizational policy & plan (i.e. governance model) exist?

212. Does the system design reflect the requirements?

213. Is the definition of the Workload Security Capabilities project scope clear; what needs to be accomplished?

214. What other teams / processes would be impacted by changes to the current process, and how?

215. Contradictory information between document sections?

216. Are there unnecessary steps that are creating bottlenecks and/or causing people to wait?

217. What does an audit system look like?

218. Have all involved stakeholders and work groups committed to the Workload Security Capabilities project?

219. What to do at recovery?

220. What do you audit?

2.8 Work Breakdown Structure: Workload Security Capabilities

221. Why would you develop a Work Breakdown Structure?

222. How far down?

223. What is the probability of completing the Workload Security Capabilities project in less that xx days?

224. How many levels?

225. What has to be done?

226. Where does it take place?

227. When does it have to be done?

228. Is the work breakdown structure (wbs) defined and is the scope of the Workload Security Capabilities project clear with assigned deliverable owners?

229. Why is it useful?

230. How big is a work-package?

231. When do you stop?

232. Is it still viable?

233. Can you make it?

234. How will you and your Workload Security Capabilities project team define the Workload Security Capabilities projects scope and work breakdown structure?

235. Who has to do it?

236. Is it a change in scope?

237. How much detail?

2.9 WBS Dictionary: Workload Security Capabilities

238. Are the latest revised estimates of costs at completion compared with the established budgets at appropriate levels and causes of variances identified?

239. Budgets assigned to control accounts?

240. Are control accounts opened and closed based on the start and completion of work contained therein?

241. Are data elements summarized through the functional organizational structure for progressively higher levels of management?

242. What is the end result of a work package?

243. Are overhead costs budgets established on a basis consistent with anticipated direct business base?

244. Performance to date and material commitment?

245. Knowledgeable Workload Security Capabilities projections of future performance?

246. Are estimates of costs at completion utilized in determining contract funding requirements and reporting them?

247. Are procedures established to prevent changes to the contract budget base other than the already stated authorized by contractual action?

248. Software specification, development, integration, and testing, licenses ?

249. What are you counting on?

250. Are there procedures for monitoring action items and corrective actions to the point of resolution and are corresponding procedures being followed?

251. Does the scheduling system provide for the identification of work progress against technical and other milestones, and also provide for forecasts of completion dates of scheduled work?

252. Is budgeted cost for work performed calculated in a manner consistent with the way work is planned?

253. Identify potential or actual budget-based and time-based schedule variances?

254. Do procedures specify under what circumstances replanning of open work packages may occur, and the methods to be followed?

255. Do the lines of authority for incurring indirect costs correspond to the lines of responsibility for management control of the same components of costs?

256. Are overhead budgets and costs being handled according to the disclosure statement when applicable, or otherwise properly classified (for

example, engineering overhead, IR&D)?

257. Are direct or indirect cost adjustments being accomplished according to accounting procedures acceptable to us?

2.10 Schedule Management Plan: Workload Security Capabilities

258. Does the business case include how the Workload Security Capabilities project aligns with your organizations strategic goals & objectives?

259. What threats might prevent you from getting there?

260. How are Workload Security Capabilities projects different from operations?

261. Are Workload Security Capabilities project leaders committed to this Workload Security Capabilities project full time?

262. Can be realistically shortened (the duration of subsequent tasks)?

263. What does a valid Schedule look like?

264. Are post milestone Workload Security Capabilities project reviews (PMPR) conducted with your organization at least once a year?

265. Cost / benefit analysis?

266. How does the proposed individual meet each requirement?

267. What weaknesses do you have?

268. Will the Workload Security Capabilities project sponsor be involved in preliminary schedule reviews?

269. Are the primary and secondary schedule tools defined?

270. Have activity relationships and interdependencies within tasks been adequately identified?

271. Are risk oriented checklists used during risk identification?

272. Workload Security Capabilities project definition & scope?

273. Are staff skills known and available for each task?

274. Who is responsible for estimating the activity durations?

275. Perform reality checks on schedules – are all tasks included?

276. Are milestone deliverables effectively tracked and compared to Workload Security Capabilities project plan?

277. Has a resource management plan been created?

2.11 Activity List: Workload Security Capabilities

278. What is your organizations history in doing similar activities?

279. How do you determine the late start (LS) for each activity?

280. How should ongoing costs be monitored to try to keep the Workload Security Capabilities project within budget?

281. Where will it be performed?

282. How will it be performed?

283. What are the critical bottleneck activities?

284. Who will perform the work?

285. Is there anything planned that does not need to be here?

286. In what sequence?

287. What is the probability the Workload Security Capabilities project can be completed in xx weeks?

288. Can you determine the activity that must finish, before this activity can start?

289. When will the work be performed?

290. What is the LF and LS for each activity?

291. The wbs is developed as part of a joint planning session. and how do you know that youhave done this right?

292. When do the individual activities need to start and finish?

293. What is the total time required to complete the Workload Security Capabilities project if no delays occur?

294. What will be performed?

2.12 Activity Attributes: Workload Security Capabilities

295. How do you manage time?

296. Where else does it apply?

297. What activity do you think you should spend the most time on?

298. How much activity detail is required?

299. How many days do you need to complete the work scope with a limit of X number of resources?

300. Were there other ways you could have organized the data to achieve similar results?

301. Can more resources be added?

302. Have constraints been applied to the start and finish milestones for the phases?

303. Activity: what is In the Bag?

304. Why?

305. Do you feel very comfortable with your prediction?

306. Can you re-assign any activities to another resource to resolve an over-allocation?

307. How many resources do you need to complete the work scope within a limit of X number of days?

308. Activity: fair or not fair?

309. What is the general pattern here?

310. Are the required resources available?

311. Which method produces the more accurate cost assignment?

2.13 Milestone List: Workload Security Capabilities

312. Own known vulnerabilities?

313. Gaps in capabilities?

314. Sustainable financial backing?

315. What would happen if a delivery of material was one week late?

316. How will you get the word out to customers?

317. Loss of key staff?

318. Milestone pages should display the UserID of the person who added the milestone. Does a report or query exist that provides this audit information?

319. Who will manage the Workload Security Capabilities project on a day-to-day basis?

320. How soon can the activity finish?

321. Calculate how long can activity be delayed?

322. What has been done so far?

323. It is to be a narrative text providing the crucial aspects of your Workload Security Capabilities project proposal answering what, who, how, when and where?

324. Which path is the critical path?

325. What background experience, skills, and strengths does the team bring to your organization?

326. Insurmountable weaknesses?

327. Usps (unique selling points)?

328. New USPs?

329. How difficult will it be to do specific activities on this Workload Security Capabilities project?

2.14 Network Diagram: Workload Security Capabilities

330. Exercise: what is the probability that the Workload Security Capabilities project duration will exceed xx weeks?

331. What are the Key Success Factors?

332. Are the gantt chart and/or network diagram updated periodically and used to assess the overall Workload Security Capabilities project timetable?

333. Why must you schedule milestones, such as reviews, throughout the Workload Security Capabilities project?

334. What activity must be completed immediately before this activity can start?

335. Planning: who, how long, what to do?

336. What is the lowest cost to complete this Workload Security Capabilities project in xx weeks?

337. What activities must occur simultaneously with this activity?

338. What are the tools?

339. What is the probability of completing the Workload Security Capabilities project in less that xx days?

340. Where do schedules come from?

341. If a current contract exists, can you provide the vendor name, contract start, and contract expiration date?

342. What to do and When?

343. What job or jobs follow it?

344. If the Workload Security Capabilities project network diagram cannot change and you have extra personnel resources, what is the BEST thing to do?

345. What job or jobs could run concurrently?

346. What is the completion time?

347. What controls the start and finish of a job?

348. Where do you schedule uncertainty time?

2.15 Activity Resource Requirements: Workload Security Capabilities

349. Organizational Applicability?

350. Why do you do that?

351. What are constraints that you might find during the Human Resource Planning process?

352. When does monitoring begin?

353. Are there unresolved issues that need to be addressed?

354. Other support in specific areas?

355. Time for overtime?

356. How do you handle petty cash?

357. Which logical relationship does the PDM use most often?

358. What is the Work Plan Standard?

359. Do you use tools like decomposition and rolling-wave planning to produce the activity list and other outputs?

360. Anything else?

361. How many signatures do you require on a

check and does this match what is in your policy and procedures?

2.16 Resource Breakdown Structure: Workload Security Capabilities

362. How should the information be delivered?

363. Who delivers the information?

364. Which resource planning tool provides information on resource responsibility and accountability?

365. Any changes from stakeholders?

366. What is the purpose of assigning and documenting responsibility?

367. What is the primary purpose of the human resource plan?

368. Who is allowed to perform which functions?

369. Which resources should be in the resource pool?

370. What can you do to improve productivity?

371. What defines a successful Workload Security Capabilities project?

372. Why is this important?

373. Who will use the system?

374. Who is allowed to see what data about which

resources?

375. What are the requirements for resource data?

376. When do they need the information?

377. What is the number one predictor of a groups productivity?

378. What is the difference between % Complete and % work?

379. What defines a successful Workload Security Capabilities project?

2.17 Activity Duration Estimates: Workload Security Capabilities

380. What do you think about the WBSs for them?

381. What is wrong with this scenario?

382. How do theories relate to Workload Security Capabilities project management?

383. How is the Workload Security Capabilities project doing?

384. Workload Security Capabilities project manager is using weighted average duration estimates to perform schedule network analysis. Which type of mathematical analysis is being used?

385. What tasks must follow this task?

386. How does the job market and current state of the economy affect human resource management?

387. Are the causes of all variances identified?

388. How many different communications channels does a Workload Security Capabilities project team with six people have?

389. What steps did your organization take to earn this prestigious quality award?

390. Are procedures defined by which the Workload

Security Capabilities project scope may be changed?

391. What time management activity should you do NEXT?

392. Are activity dependencies identified?

393. Do stakeholders follow a procedure for formally accepting the Workload Security Capabilities project scope?

394. Do an internet search on earning pmp certification. be sure to search for yahoo groups related to this topic. what are the options you found to help people prepare for the exam?

395. Consider the history of modern quality management. How have experts such as Deming, Juran, Crosby, and Taguchi affected the quality movement and todays use of Six Sigma?

396. What are the Workload Security Capabilities project management deliverables of each process group?

397. What is the critical path for this Workload Security Capabilities project and how long is it?

2.18 Duration Estimating Worksheet: Workload Security Capabilities

398. When, then?

399. What is your role?

400. Why estimate costs?

401. What work will be included in the Workload Security Capabilities project?

402. What is an Average Workload Security Capabilities project?

403. Why estimate time and cost?

404. Does the Workload Security Capabilities project provide innovative ways for stakeholders to overcome obstacles or deliver better outcomes?

405. Do any colleagues have experience with your organization and/or RFPs?

406. What utility impacts are there?

407. What questions do you have?

408. How should ongoing costs be monitored to try to keep the Workload Security Capabilities project within budget?

409. Can the Workload Security Capabilities project be

constructed as planned?

410. Is this operation cost effective?

411. Will the Workload Security Capabilities project collaborate with the local community and leverage resources?

412. Small or large Workload Security Capabilities project?

413. When does your organization expect to be able to complete it?

414. How can the Workload Security Capabilities project be displayed graphically to better visualize the activities?

2.19 Project Schedule: Workload Security Capabilities

415. Are procedures defined by which the Workload Security Capabilities project schedule may be changed?

416. Should you have a test for each code module?

417. Schedule/cost recovery?

418. Meet requirements?

419. Why do you need to manage Workload Security Capabilities project Risk?

420. It allows the Workload Security Capabilities project to be delivered on schedule. How Do you Use Schedules?

421. How effectively were issues able to be resolved without impacting the Workload Security Capabilities project Schedule or Budget?

422. Verify that the update is accurate. Are all remaining durations correct?

423. Are all remaining durations correct?

424. How can you minimize or control changes to Workload Security Capabilities project schedules?

425. Was the Workload Security Capabilities project

schedule reviewed by all stakeholders and formally accepted?

426. How do you know that youhave done this right?

427. Did the Workload Security Capabilities project come in on schedule?

428. What is the most mis-scheduled part of process?

429. Workload Security Capabilities project work estimates Who is managing the work estimate quality of work tasks in the Workload Security Capabilities project schedule?

430. What is Workload Security Capabilities project management?

431. Activity charts and bar charts are graphical representations of a Workload Security Capabilities project schedule ...how do they differ?

2.20 Cost Management Plan: Workload Security Capabilities

432. Cost estimate preparation – What cost estimates will be prepared during the Workload Security Capabilities project phases?

433. What is cost and Workload Security Capabilities project cost management?

434. Contingency rundown curve be used on the Workload Security Capabilities project?

435. Have external dependencies been captured in the schedule?

436. Are the quality tools and methods identified in the Quality Plan appropriate to the Workload Security Capabilities project?

437. Is your organization certified as a supplier, wholesaler, regular dealer, or manufacturer of corresponding products/supplies?

438. Does the business case include how the Workload Security Capabilities project aligns with your organizations strategic goals & objectives?

439. Workload Security Capabilities project Objectives?

440. Contingency – how will cost contingency be administered?

441. Is the Workload Security Capabilities project schedule available for all Workload Security Capabilities project team members to review?

442. Does the schedule include Workload Security Capabilities project management time and change request analysis time?

443. Schedule contingency – how will the schedule contingency be administrated?

444. Is there an issues management plan in place?

445. Is current scope of the Workload Security Capabilities project substantially different than that originally defined?

446. Sensitivity analysis?

447. Are vendor contract reports, reviews and visits conducted periodically?

448. Exclusions – is there scope to be performed or provided by others?

449. Has the business need been clearly defined?

450. Are decisions captured in a decisions log?

451. Is there a requirements change management processes in place?

2.21 Activity Cost Estimates: Workload Security Capabilities

452. What is the estimators estimating history?

453. Based on your Workload Security Capabilities project communication management plan, what worked well?

454. Maintenance Reserve?

455. If you are asked to lower your estimate because the price is too high, what are your options?

456. Did the Workload Security Capabilities project team have the right skills?

457. How do you allocate indirect costs to activities?

458. How do you change activities?

459. Who determines the quality and expertise of contractors?

460. Does the activity serve a common type of customer?

461. Would you hire them again?

462. One way to define activities is to consider how organization employees describe jobs to families and friends. You basically want to know, What do you do?

463. Does the estimator have experience?

464. Were sponsors and decision makers available when needed outside regularly scheduled meetings?

465. What is included in indirect cost being allocated?

466. Where can you get activity reports?

467. Were decisions made in a timely manner?

468. What are you looking for?

469. How do you treat administrative costs in the activity inventory?

470. Performance bond should always provide what part of the contract value?

471. What makes a good activity description?

2.22 Cost Estimating Worksheet: Workload Security Capabilities

472. Does the Workload Security Capabilities project provide innovative ways for stakeholders to overcome obstacles or deliver better outcomes?

473. How will the results be shared and to whom?

474. What can be included?

475. Is the Workload Security Capabilities project responsive to community need?

476. What is the purpose of estimating?

477. Identify the timeframe necessary to monitor progress and collect data to determine how the selected measure has changed?

478. What additional Workload Security Capabilities project(s) could be initiated as a result of this Workload Security Capabilities project?

479. Value pocket identification & quantification what are value pockets?

480. Who is best positioned to know and assist in identifying corresponding factors?

481. Is it feasible to establish a control group arrangement?

482. Will the Workload Security Capabilities project collaborate with the local community and leverage resources?

483. What happens to any remaining funds not used?

484. Ask: are others positioned to know, are others credible, and will others cooperate?

485. What info is needed?

486. Can a trend be established from historical performance data on the selected measure and are the criteria for using trend analysis or forecasting methods met?

487. What will others want?

488. What is the estimated labor cost today based upon this information?

489. What costs are to be estimated?

2.23 Cost Baseline: Workload Security Capabilities

490. What does a good WBS NOT look like?

491. Who will use corresponding metrics ?

492. Has the documentation relating to operation and maintenance of the product(s) or service(s) been delivered to, and accepted by, operations management?

493. What would the life cycle costs be?

494. Has the actual cost of the Workload Security Capabilities project (or Workload Security Capabilities project phase) been tallied and compared to the approved budget?

495. Does it impact schedule, cost, quality?

496. What do you want to measure ?

497. For what purpose ?

498. How will cost estimates be used?

499. Will the Workload Security Capabilities project fail if the change request is not executed?

500. How likely is it to go wrong?

501. Verify business objectives. Are others

appropriate, and well-articulated?

502. Pcs for your new business. what would the life cycle costs be?

503. Are there contingencies or conditions related to the acceptance?

504. Does the suggested change request seem to represent a necessary enhancement to the product?

505. Have the actual milestone completion dates been compared to the approved schedule?

506. What can go wrong?

507. Have the lessons learned been filed with the Workload Security Capabilities project Management Office?

2.24 Quality Management Plan: Workload Security Capabilities

508. Contradictory information between different documents?

509. Written by multiple authors and in multiple writing styles?

510. How are records kept in the office?

511. How will you know that a change is actually an improvement?

512. What is quality and how will you ensure it?

513. How is the information recorded?

514. Diagrams and tables to account for complex concepts and increase overall readability?

515. How are people conducting sampling trained?

516. How are changes approved?

517. When reporting to different audiences, do you vary the form or type of report?

518. Are you meeting your customers expectations consistently?

519. Where do you focus?

520. How are changes recorded?

521. How are changes to procedures made?

522. Have all involved stakeholders and work groups committed to the Workload Security Capabilities project?

523. How are calibration records kept?

524. How long do you retain data?

525. How do you ensure that your sampling methods and procedures meet your data needs?

2.25 Quality Metrics: Workload Security Capabilities

526. Are quality metrics defined?

527. What documentation is required?

528. Are applicable standards referenced and available?

529. Has risk analysis been adequately reviewed?

530. Who notifies stakeholders of normal and abnormal results?

531. Where is quality now?

532. How do you know if everyone is trying to improve the right things?

533. What metrics are important and most beneficial to measure?

534. What are you trying to accomplish?

535. The metrics–what is being considered?

536. Filter visualizations of interest?

537. Did the team meet the Workload Security Capabilities project success criteria documented in the Quality Metrics Matrix?

538. What do you measure?

539. How do you measure?

540. When will the Final Guidance will be issued?

541. What is the timeline to meet your goal?

542. How effective are your security tests?

543. How do you communicate results and findings to upper management?

544. What happens if you get an abnormal result?

2.26 Process Improvement Plan: Workload Security Capabilities

545. Are you following the quality standards?

546. Purpose of goal: the motive is determined by asking, why do you want to achieve this goal?

547. Has the time line required to move measurement results from the points of collection to databases or users been established?

548. What actions are needed to address the problems and achieve the goals?

549. What personnel are the sponsors for that initiative?

550. Where do you want to be?

551. Modeling current processes is great, and will you ever see a return on that investment?

552. Are you making progress on the goals?

553. Management commitment at all levels?

554. To elicit goal statements, do you ask a question such as, What do you want to achieve?

555. Have storage and access mechanisms and procedures been determined?

556. Are you meeting the quality standards?

557. What personnel are the change agents for your initiative?

558. Are you making progress on your improvement plan?

559. What lessons have you learned so far?

560. Why do you want to achieve the goal?

561. How do you manage quality?

562. Where are you now?

2.27 Responsibility Assignment Matrix: Workload Security Capabilities

563. Actual cost of work performed?

564. Does the contractors system include procedures for measuring the performance of critical subcontractors?

565. The already stated responsible for the establishment of budgets and assignment of resources for overhead performance?

566. What cost control tool do many experts say is crucial to Workload Security Capabilities project management?

567. Contemplated overhead expenditure for each period based on the best information currently available?

568. Budgets assigned to major functional organizations?

569. Are others working on the right things?

570. Are the bases and rates for allocating costs from each indirect pool consistently applied?

571. Is data disseminated to the contractors management timely, accurate, and usable?

572. The anticipated business volume?

573. Are records maintained to show how management reserves are used?

574. How do you assist them to be as productive as possible?

575. Is the entire contract planned in time-phased control accounts to the extent practicable?

576. Workload Security Capabilities projected economic escalation?

577. What do you do when people do not respond?

578. Who is responsible for work and budgets for each wbs?

579. Where does all this information come from?

2.28 Roles and Responsibilities: Workload Security Capabilities

580. What areas of supervision are challenging for you?

581. Have you ever been a part of this team?

582. What should you do now to prepare yourself for a promotion, increased responsibilities or a different job?

583. Be specific; avoid generalities. Thank you and great work alone are insufficient. What exactly do you appreciate and why?

584. What is working well within your organizations performance management system?

585. What should you do now to ensure that you are meeting all expectations of your current position?

586. Concern: where are you limited or have no authority, where you can not influence?

587. Once the responsibilities are defined for the Workload Security Capabilities project, have the deliverables, roles and responsibilities been clearly communicated to every participant?

588. Are governance roles and responsibilities documented?

589. Are Workload Security Capabilities project team roles and responsibilities identified and documented?

590. What is working well?

591. What should you do now to prepare for your career 5+ years from now?

592. Who is responsible for implementation activities and where will the functions, roles and responsibilities be defined?

593. Is the data complete?

594. How is your work-life balance?

595. Do the values and practices inherent in the culture of your organization foster or hinder the process?

596. Who is responsible for each task?

597. Where are you most strong as a supervisor?

598. Does the team have access to and ability to use data analysis tools?

599. What should you highlight for improvement?

2.29 Human Resource Management Plan: Workload Security Capabilities

600. Are Workload Security Capabilities project team members committed fulltime?

601. List the assumptions made to date. What did you have to assume to be true to complete the charter?

602. Does all Workload Security Capabilities project documentation reside in a common repository for easy access?

603. Do Workload Security Capabilities project managers participating in the Workload Security Capabilities project know the Workload Security Capabilities projects true status first hand?

604. Who will be impacted (both positively and negatively) as a result of or during the execution of this Workload Security Capabilities project?

605. Were stakeholders aware and supportive of the principles and practices of modern cost estimation?

606. Does the resource management plan include a personnel development plan?

607. Is the quality assurance team identified?

608. Is the manpower level sufficient to meet the future business requirements?

609. Are the schedule estimates reasonable given the Workload Security Capabilities project?

610. Have Workload Security Capabilities project team accountabilities & responsibilities been clearly defined?

611. Have stakeholder accountabilities & responsibilities been clearly defined?

612. Are the Workload Security Capabilities project plans updated on a frequent basis?

613. Who is involved?

614. Is there a formal set of procedures supporting Stakeholder Management?

615. Are cause and effect determined for risks when others occur?

616. Is there an onboarding process in place?

2.30 Communications Management Plan: Workload Security Capabilities

617. Conflict resolution -which method when?

618. How did the term stakeholder originate?

619. What data is going to be required?

620. What to know?

621. How much time does it take to do it?

622. How do you manage communications?

623. Who to learn from?

624. What approaches do you use?

625. What communications method?

626. Do you have members of your team responsible for certain stakeholders?

627. What to learn?

628. How is this initiative related to other portfolios, programs, or Workload Security Capabilities projects?

629. Which stakeholders can influence others?

630. Who did you turn to if you had questions?

631. Will messages be directly related to the release strategy or phases of the Workload Security Capabilities project?

632. Do you feel more overwhelmed by stakeholders?

633. What is the political influence?

634. Which team member will work with each stakeholder?

635. Who to share with?

2.31 Risk Management Plan: Workload Security Capabilities

636. Do you have a mechanism for managing change?

637. What can you do to minimize the impact if it does?

638. What is the likelihood that your organization would accept responsibility for the risk?

639. Is Workload Security Capabilities project scope stable?

640. How can you fix it?

641. Are you working on the right risks?

642. Litigation – what is the probability that lawsuits will cause problems or delays in the Workload Security Capabilities project?

643. Why might it be late?

644. Is the necessary data being captured and is it complete and accurate?

645. What will drive change?

646. Does the customer have a solid idea of what is required?

647. Have customers been involved fully in the

definition of requirements?

648. Market risk: will the new product be useful to your organization or marketable to others?

649. Are enough people available?

650. Are requirements fully understood by the software engineering team and customers?

651. For software; are compilers and code generators available and suitable for the product to be built?

652. Does the software engineering team have the right mix of skills?

653. Why do you need to manage Workload Security Capabilities project Risk?

654. People risk -are people with appropriate skills available to help complete the Workload Security Capabilities project?

655. What are the chances the event will occur?

2.32 Risk Register: Workload Security Capabilities

656. How could corresponding Risk affect the Workload Security Capabilities project in terms of cost and schedule?

657. Methodology: how will risk management be performed on this Workload Security Capabilities project?

658. Are there any knock-on effects/impact on any of the other areas?

659. What will be done?

660. People risk -are people with appropriate skills available to help complete the Workload Security Capabilities project?

661. What could prevent you delivering on the strategic program objectives and what is being done to mitigate corresponding issues?

662. Risk categories: what are the main categories of risks that should be addressed on this Workload Security Capabilities project?

663. Who needs to know about this?

664. What may happen or not go according to plan?

665. When would you develop a risk register?

666. Manageability – have mitigations to the risk been identified?

667. Are there other alternative controls that could be implemented?

668. What are the major risks facing the Workload Security Capabilities project?

669. How often will the Risk Management Plan and Risk Register be formally reviewed, and by whom?

670. Preventative actions - planned actions to reduce the likelihood a risk will occur and/or reduce the seriousness should it occur. What should you do now?

671. What has changed since the last period?

672. What evidence do you have to justify the likelihood score of the risk (audit, incident report, claim, complaints, inspection, internal review)?

673. What further options might be available for responding to the risk?

2.33 Probability and Impact Assessment: Workload Security Capabilities

674. How well is the risk understood?

675. Have you ascribed a level of confidence to every critical technical objective?

676. Risk urgency assessment -which of your risks could occur soon, or require a longer planning time?

677. Costs associated with late delivery or a defective product?

678. What are your data sources?

679. What significant shift will occur in governmental policies, laws, and regulations pertaining to specific industries?

680. Have decisions that should be left open because of inadequate information on technology been identified and responsibility assigned for reducing the uncertainty?

681. Do requirements demand the use of new analysis, design, or testing methods?

682. Are there any Workload Security Capabilities projects similar to this one in existence?

683. Assumptions analysis -what assumptions have

you made or been given about your Workload Security Capabilities project?

684. Are the risk data timely and relevant?

685. How much risk do others need to take?

686. Are the best people available?

687. What should be the gestation period for the Workload Security Capabilities project with specific technology?

688. What would be the effect of slippage?

689. Supply/demand Workload Security Capabilities projections and trends; what are the levels of accuracy?

690. What will be the likely political environment during the life of the Workload Security Capabilities project?

691. Do you have a consistent repeatable process that is actually used?

692. Your customers business requirements have suddenly shifted because of a new regulatory statute, what now?

2.34 Probability and Impact Matrix: Workload Security Capabilities

693. What are the risks involved in appointing external agencies to manage the Workload Security Capabilities project?

694. Which is an input to the risk management process?

695. Have staff received necessary training?

696. Do you need a risk management plan?

697. Economic to take on the Workload Security Capabilities project?

698. Mandated specific features?

699. What are the current or emerging trends of culture?

700. Do end-users have realistic expectations?

701. Maximize short-term return on investment?

702. What are ways to measure and evaluate risks?

703. Is the delay in one subWorkload Security Capabilities project going to affect another?

704. Do you use any methods to analyze risks?

705. Mitigation -how can you avoid the risk?

706. Which risks need to move on to Perform Quantitative Risk Analysis?

707. How do you manage Workload Security Capabilities project Risk?

708. Do requirements put excessive performance constraints on the product?

709. What are its business ethics?

710. Are flexibility and reuse paramount?

2.35 Risk Data Sheet: Workload Security Capabilities

711. How do you handle product safely?

712. What was measured?

713. What is the chance that it will happen?

714. How reliable is the data source?

715. During work activities could hazards exist?

716. What are the main opportunities available to you that you should grab while you can?

717. What can happen?

718. What do you know?

719. What will be the consequences if the risk happens?

720. Do effective diagnostic tests exist?

721. What are you trying to achieve (Objectives)?

722. What is the likelihood of it happening?

723. Are new hazards created?

724. Whom do you serve (customers)?

725. What will be the consequences if it happens?

726. Type of risk identified?

727. How can it happen?

728. Who has a vested interest in how you perform as your organization (our stakeholders)?

729. What were the Causes that contributed?

2.36 Procurement Management Plan: Workload Security Capabilities

730. Are updated Workload Security Capabilities project time & resource estimates reasonable based on the current Workload Security Capabilities project stage?

731. Have lessons learned been conducted after each Workload Security Capabilities project release?

732. How will you coordinate Procurement with aspects of the Workload Security Capabilities project?

733. Is Workload Security Capabilities project work proceeding in accordance with the original Workload Security Capabilities project schedule?

734. What areas does the group agree are the biggest success on the Workload Security Capabilities project?

735. Are Workload Security Capabilities project leaders committed to this Workload Security Capabilities project full time?

736. Are key risk mitigation strategies added to the Workload Security Capabilities project schedule?

737. What were things that you did well, and could improve, and how?

738. Does all Workload Security Capabilities project documentation reside in a common repository for

easy access?

739. Have Workload Security Capabilities project management standards and procedures been identified / established and documented?

740. How will multiple providers be managed?

741. Are actuals compared against estimates to analyze and correct variances?

742. In which phase of the Acquisition Process Cycle does source qualifications reside?

743. Are the Workload Security Capabilities project plans updated on a frequent basis?

744. Are milestone deliverables effectively tracked and compared to Workload Security Capabilities project plan?

745. Are post milestone Workload Security Capabilities project reviews (PMPR) conducted with your organization at least once a year?

746. If independent estimates will be needed as evaluation criteria, who will prepare them and when?

747. Is there an on-going process in place to monitor Workload Security Capabilities project risks?

748. Are Workload Security Capabilities project contact logs kept up to date?

2.37 Source Selection Criteria: Workload Security Capabilities

749. How can solicitation Schedules be improved to yield more effective price competition?

750. How much past performance information should be requested?

751. What should communications be used to accomplish?

752. What procedures are followed when a contractor requires access to classified information or a significant quantity of special material/information?

753. What should clarifications include?

754. Do you consider all weaknesses, significant weaknesses, and deficiencies?

755. What risks were identified in the proposals?

756. Is the offeror pricing what is technically proposed?

757. Are they compliant with all technical requirements?

758. How do you consolidate reviews and analysis of evaluators?

759. Are resultant proposal revisions allowed?

760. Are evaluators ready to begin this task?

761. When must you conduct a debriefing?

762. How do you ensure an integrated assessment of proposals?

763. What documentation is necessary regarding electronic communications?

764. How should the solicitation aspects regarding past performance be structured?

765. What is the basis of an estimate and what assumptions were made?

766. Are responses to considerations adequate?

767. Has all proposal data been loaded?

768. What should preproposal conferences accomplish?

2.38 Stakeholder Management Plan: Workload Security Capabilities

769. Who is gathering information?

770. Is pert / critical path or equivalent methodology being used?

771. Has a Workload Security Capabilities project Communications Plan been developed?

772. Are the Workload Security Capabilities project team members located locally to the users/ stakeholders?

773. Is there an on-going process in place to monitor Workload Security Capabilities project risks?

774. Are non-critical path items updated and agreed upon with the teams?

775. Have reserves been created to address risks?

776. Are best practices and metrics employed to identify issues, progress, performance, etc.?

777. What potential impact does the stakeholder have on the Workload Security Capabilities project?

778. Are mitigation strategies identified?

779. Are the Workload Security Capabilities project plans updated on a frequent basis?

780. Have all team members been part of identifying risks?

781. Detail warranty and/or maintenance periods?

782. Has the budget been baselined?

783. What are reporting requirements?

784. Has the Workload Security Capabilities project manager been identified?

785. Are Workload Security Capabilities project team members committed fulltime?

2.39 Change Management Plan: Workload Security Capabilities

786. What skills, education, knowledge, or work experiences should the resources have for each identified competency?

787. Have the approved procedures and policies been published?

788. Who might present the most resistance?

789. What policies and procedures need to be changed?

790. Are there any restrictions on who can receive the communications?

791. Has the relevant business unit been notified of installation and support requirements?

792. When does it make sense to customize?

793. What would be an estimate of the total cost for the activities required to carry out the change initiative?

794. What work practices will be affected?

795. Do there need to be new channels developed?

796. What do you expect the target audience to do, say, think or feel as a result of this communication?

797. Who is the target audience of the piece of information?

798. What provokes organizational change?

799. What risks may occur upfront?

800. How does the principle of senders and receivers make the Workload Security Capabilities project communications effort more complex?

801. How might they respond to the message and if the response may be negative or open to misinterpretation, what else needs to be said?

802. Would you need to tailor a special message for each segment of the audience?

803. What roles within your organization are affected, and how?

804. How can you best frame the message so that it addresses the audiences interests?

3.0 Executing Process Group: Workload Security Capabilities

805. How well defined and documented were the Workload Security Capabilities project management processes you chose to use?

806. Is the program supported by national and/or local organizations?

807. How well did the chosen processes fit the needs of the Workload Security Capabilities project?

808. Will additional funds be needed for hardware or software?

809. How do you measure difficulty?

810. Who are the Workload Security Capabilities project stakeholders?

811. What are the critical steps involved with strategy mapping?

812. What is the shortest possible time it will take to complete this Workload Security Capabilities project?

813. What good practices or successful experiences or transferable examples have been identified?

814. How well did the team follow the chosen processes?

815. What are the main types of goods and services being outsourced?

816. How will professionals learn what is expected from them what the deliverables are?

817. Who will be the main sponsor?

818. Why is it important to determine activity sequencing on Workload Security Capabilities projects?

819. Based on your Workload Security Capabilities project communication management plan, what worked well?

820. What will you do to minimize the impact should a risk event occur?

821. How do you prevent staff are just doing busywork to pass the time?

822. What is the critical path for this Workload Security Capabilities project and how long is it?

823. How does a Workload Security Capabilities project life cycle differ from a product life cycle?

824. Why should Workload Security Capabilities project managers strive to make jobs look easy?

3.1 Team Member Status Report: Workload Security Capabilities

825. Will the staff do training or is that done by a third party?

826. Are the attitudes of staff regarding Workload Security Capabilities project work improving?

827. Does every department have to have a Workload Security Capabilities project Manager on staff?

828. How does this product, good, or service meet the needs of the Workload Security Capabilities project and your organization as a whole?

829. How much risk is involved?

830. The problem with Reward & Recognition Programs is that the truly deserving people all too often get left out. How can you make it practical?

831. Does the product, good, or service already exist within your organization?

832. What is to be done?

833. Is there evidence that staff is taking a more professional approach toward management of your organizations Workload Security Capabilities projects?

834. Does your organization have the means (staff, money, contract, etc.) to produce or to acquire the

product, good, or service?

835. When a teams productivity and success depend on collaboration and the efficient flow of information, what generally fails them?

836. How it is to be done?

837. Are your organizations Workload Security Capabilities projects more successful over time?

838. How can you make it practical?

839. Are the products of your organizations Workload Security Capabilities projects meeting customers objectives?

840. What specific interest groups do you have in place?

841. How will resource planning be done?

842. Do you have an Enterprise Workload Security Capabilities project Management Office (EPMO)?

843. Why is it to be done?

3.2 Change Request: Workload Security Capabilities

844. Who is responsible for the implementation and monitoring of all measures?

845. For which areas does this operating procedure apply?

846. How do you get changes (code) out in a timely manner?

847. Are there requirements attributes that are strongly related to the occurrence of defects and failures?

848. What are the requirements for urgent changes?

849. Will new change requests be acknowledged in a timely manner?

850. Who will perform the change?

851. Who can suggest changes?

852. What needs to be communicated?

853. How can you ensure that changes have been made properly?

854. Why control change across the life cycle?

855. Should staff call into the helpdesk or go to the

website?

856. Since there are no change requests in your Workload Security Capabilities project at this point, what must you have before you begin?

857. Can static requirements change attributes like the size of the change be used to predict reliability in execution?

858. What are the basic mechanics of the Change Advisory Board (CAB)?

859. What mechanism is used to appraise others of changes that are made?

860. What can be filed?

861. How fast will change requests be approved?

862. What is the function of the change control committee?

863. What are the duties of the change control team?

3.3 Change Log: Workload Security Capabilities

864. Do the described changes impact on the integrity or security of the system?

865. Should a more thorough impact analysis be conducted?

866. When was the request submitted?

867. Is the change backward compatible without limitations?

868. Is the change request within Workload Security Capabilities project scope?

869. Is the submitted change a new change or a modification of a previously approved change?

870. Where do changes come from?

871. Does the suggested change request represent a desired enhancement to the products functionality?

872. Is this a mandatory replacement?

873. Who initiated the change request?

874. How does this change affect the timeline of the schedule?

875. How does this change affect scope?

876. When was the request approved?

877. Is the requested change request a result of changes in other Workload Security Capabilities project(s)?

878. Is the change request open, closed or pending?

879. Will the Workload Security Capabilities project fail if the change request is not executed?

880. How does this relate to the standards developed for specific business processes?

3.4 Decision Log: Workload Security Capabilities

881. Who is the decisionmaker?

882. What alternatives/risks were considered?

883. What is your overall strategy for quality control / quality assurance procedures?

884. With whom was the decision shared or considered?

885. Who will be given a copy of this document and where will it be kept?

886. Does anything need to be adjusted?

887. How does provision of information, both in terms of content and presentation, influence acceptance of alternative strategies?

888. How does the use a Decision Support System influence the strategies/tactics or costs?

889. What was the rationale for the decision?

890. Adversarial environment. is your opponent open to a non-traditional workflow, or will it likely challenge anything you do?

891. What eDiscovery problem or issue did your organization set out to fix or make better?

892. Decision-making process; how will the team make decisions?

893. At what point in time does loss become unacceptable?

894. Behaviors; what are guidelines that the team has identified that will assist them with getting the most out of team meetings?

895. Linked to original objective?

896. It becomes critical to track and periodically revisit both operational effectiveness; Are you noticing all that you need to, and are you interpreting what you see effectively?

897. Do strategies and tactics aimed at less than full control reduce the costs of management or simply shift the cost burden?

898. Is your opponent open to a non-traditional workflow, or will it likely challenge anything you do?

899. How does an increasing emphasis on cost containment influence the strategies and tactics used?

900. What is the line where eDiscovery ends and document review begins?

3.5 Quality Audit: Workload Security Capabilities

901. How does your organization know that its quality of teaching is appropriately effective and constructive?

902. It is inappropriate to seek information about the Audit Panels preliminary views including questions like why do you ask that?

903. How does your organization know that its relationships with industry and employers are appropriately effective and constructive?

904. How does your organization know that it provides a safe and healthy environment?

905. Have personnel cleanliness and health requirements been established?

906. How does your organization know that its staff placements are appropriately effective and constructive in relation to program-related learning outcomes?

907. How does your organization know that the support for its staff is appropriately effective and constructive?

908. What data about organizational performance is routinely collected and reported?

909. How does your organization know that its system for staff performance planning and review is appropriately effective and constructive?

910. How does your organization know that the range and quality of its accommodation, catering and transportation services are appropriately effective and constructive?

911. How does your organization know that its systems for communicating with and among staff are appropriately effective and constructive?

912. Do prior clients have a positive opinion of your organization?

913. What experience do staff have in the type of work that the audit entails?

914. Are all areas associated with the storage and reconditioning of devices clean, free of rubbish, adequately ventilated and in good repair?

915. How does your organization know that its staff financial services are appropriately effective and constructive?

916. How does your organization know that its staff embody the core knowledge, skills and characteristics for which it wishes to be recognized?

917. What mechanisms exist for identification of staff development needs?

918. Is refuse and garbage adequately stored and disposed of with sufficient frequency to prevent

contamination?

919. What does an analysis of your organizations staff profile suggest in terms of its planning, and how is this being addressed?

920. Is there a risk that information provided by management may not always be reliable?

3.6 Team Directory: Workload Security Capabilities

921. Who will talk to the customer?

922. Have you decided when to celebrate the Workload Security Capabilities projects completion date?

923. Decisions: is the most suitable form of contract being used?

924. Process decisions: which organizational elements and which individuals will be assigned management functions?

925. How will the team handle changes?

926. Who will write the meeting minutes and distribute?

927. When does information need to be distributed?

928. Where should the information be distributed?

929. Process decisions: are all start-up, turn over and close out requirements of the contract satisfied?

930. Does a Workload Security Capabilities project team directory list all resources assigned to the Workload Security Capabilities project?

931. Who will report Workload Security Capabilities

project status to all stakeholders?

932. Process decisions: do invoice amounts match accepted work in place?

933. Why is the work necessary?

934. Who is the Sponsor?

935. Process decisions: do job conditions warrant additional actions to collect job information and document on-site activity?

936. Process decisions: are there any statutory or regulatory issues relevant to the timely execution of work?

937. Who are the Team Members?

938. How do unidentified risks impact the outcome of the Workload Security Capabilities project?

3.7 Team Operating Agreement: Workload Security Capabilities

939. Are team roles clearly defined and accepted?

940. Reimbursements: how will the team members be reimbursed for expenses and time commitments?

941. What went well?

942. Do you listen for voice tone and word choice to understand the meaning behind words?

943. Did you recap the meeting purpose, time, and expectations?

944. Must your team members rely on the expertise of other members to complete tasks?

945. What is the number of cases currently teamed?

946. Is compensation based on team and individual performance?

947. Do you ensure that all participants know how to use the required technology?

948. How will your group handle planned absences?

949. Has the appropriate access to relevant data and analysis capability been granted?

950. Resource allocation: how will individual team

members account for time and expenses, and how will this be allocated in the team budget?

951. Do you solicit member feedback about meetings and what would make them better?

952. Did you determine the technology methods that best match the messages to be communicated?

953. Are leadership responsibilities shared among team members (versus a single leader)?

954. What are the current caseload numbers in the unit?

955. Does your team need access to all documents and information at all times?

956. Do you record meetings for the already stated unable to attend?

957. Are there more than two functional areas represented by your team?

958. Do you determine the meeting length and time of day?

3.8 Team Performance Assessment: Workload Security Capabilities

959. Which situations call for a more extreme type of adaptiveness in which team members actually re-define roles?

960. To what degree is there a sense that only the team can succeed?

961. How do you recognize and praise members for contributions?

962. To what degree are fresh input and perspectives systematically caught and added (for example, through information and analysis, new members, and senior sponsors)?

963. To what degree are the teams goals and objectives clear, simple, and measurable?

964. What makes opportunities more or less obvious?

965. When does the medium matter?

966. To what degree are the skill areas critical to team performance present?

967. To what degree does the teams approach to its work allow for modification and improvement over time?

968. To what degree are corresponding categories of

skills either actually or potentially represented across the membership?

969. When a reviewer complains about method variance, what is the essence of the complaint?

970. What are you doing specifically to develop the leaders around you?

971. Individual task proficiency and team process behavior: what is important for team functioning?

972. How do you manage human resources?

973. How does Workload Security Capabilities project termination impact Workload Security Capabilities project team members?

974. To what degree are the goals ambitious?

975. Effects of crew composition on crew performance: Does the whole equal the sum of its parts?

976. To what degree does the teams work approach provide opportunity for members to engage in results-based evaluation?

977. To what degree do team members agree with the goals, relative importance, and the ways in which achievement will be measured?

978. Where to from here?

3.9 Team Member Performance Assessment: Workload Security Capabilities

979. In what areas would you like to concentrate your knowledge and resources?

980. To what degree does the team possess adequate membership to achieve its ends?

981. How is your organizations Strategic Management System tied to performance measurement?

982. Does the rater (supervisor) have the authority or responsibility to tell an employee that the employees performance is unsatisfactory?

983. To what degree is the team cognizant of small wins to be celebrated along the way?

984. To what degree do members articulate the goals beyond the team membership?

985. Which training platform formats (i.e., mobile, virtual, videogame-based) were implemented in your effort(s)?

986. What types of learning are targeted (e.g., cognitive, affective, psychomotor, procedural)?

987. How do you work together to improve teaching and learning?

988. To what degree do team members understand one anothers roles and skills?

989. What is the target group for instruction (e.g., individual and collective or small team instruction)?

990. What is a general description of the processes under performance measurement and assessment?

991. How are assessments designed, delivered, and otherwise used to maximize training?

992. Why do performance reviews?

993. To what degree are the goals realistic?

994. To what extent did the evaluation influence the instructional path, such as with adaptive testing?

995. New skills/knowledge gained this year?

996. To what degree do team members frequently explore the teams purpose and its implications?

997. Is it critical or vital to the job?

3.10 Issue Log: Workload Security Capabilities

998. Why multiple evaluators?

999. Why do you manage human resources?

1000. Do you feel a register helps?

1001. What would have to change?

1002. What is a change?

1003. Is access to the Issue Log controlled?

1004. Who are the members of the governing body?

1005. What is the impact on the Business Case?

1006. What is the stakeholders level of authority?

1007. What is the status of the issue?

1008. Is the issue log kept in a safe place?

1009. What is the impact on the risks?

1010. Are stakeholder roles recognized by your organization?

1011. Are there potential barriers between the team and the stakeholder?

1012. Who reported the issue?

1013. What approaches to you feel are the best ones to use?

4.0 Monitoring and Controlling Process Group: Workload Security Capabilities

1014. Did it work?

1015. Are the necessary foundations in place to ensure the sustainability of the results of the programme?

1016. How is agile portfolio management done?

1017. Where is the Risk in the Workload Security Capabilities project?

1018. If a risk event occurs, what will you do?

1019. What were things that you did very well and want to do the same again on the next Workload Security Capabilities project?

1020. Propriety: who needs to be involved in the evaluation to be ethical?

1021. Who needs to be engaged upfront to ensure use of results?

1022. What are the goals of the program?

1023. What departments are involved in its daily operation?

1024. Use: how will they use the information?

1025. What resources (both financial and non-financial) are available/needed?

1026. What resources are necessary?

1027. Is it what was agreed upon?

1028. Are the services being delivered?

1029. What kinds of things in particular are you looking for data on?

1030. Measurable - are the targets measurable?

1031. Purpose: toward what end is the evaluation being conducted?

4.1 Project Performance Report: Workload Security Capabilities

1032. To what degree can team members vigorously define the teams purpose in considerations with others who are not part of the functioning team?

1033. To what degree will the team ensure that all members equitably share the work essential to the success of the team?

1034. What is the degree to which rules govern information exchange between individuals within your organization?

1035. To what degree does the information network provide individuals with the information they require?

1036. To what degree do team members articulate the teams work approach?

1037. To what degree will team members, individually and collectively, commit time to help themselves and others learn and develop skills?

1038. To what degree can team members meet frequently enough to accomplish the teams ends?

1039. To what degree can the team measure progress against specific goals?

1040. To what degree do the goals specify concrete team work products?

1041. To what degree do the structures of the formal organization motivate taskrelevant behavior and facilitate task completion?

1042. To what degree do team members feel that the purpose of the team is important, if not exciting?

1043. To what degree will the approach capitalize on and enhance the skills of all team members in a manner that takes into consideration other demands on members of the team?

1044. To what degree does the teams purpose constitute a broader, deeper aspiration than just accomplishing short-term goals?

1045. To what degree do the relationships of the informal organization motivate taskrelevant behavior and facilitate task completion?

1046. To what degree will each member have the opportunity to advance his or her professional skills in all three of the above categories while contributing to the accomplishment of the teams purpose and goals?

1047. To what degree are the tasks requirements reflected in the flow and storage of information?

1048. To what degree do all members feel responsible for all agreed-upon measures?

4.2 Variance Analysis: Workload Security Capabilities

1049. What is the dollar amount of the fluctuation?

1050. Are there changes in the direct base to which overhead costs are allocated?

1051. Wbs elements contractually specified for reporting of status to your organization (lowest level only)?

1052. Are your organizations and items of cost assigned to each pool identified?

1053. Does the accounting system provide a basis for auditing records of direct costs chargeable to the contract?

1054. Are detailed work packages planned as far in advance as practicable?

1055. Are overhead cost budgets established for each department which has authority to incur overhead costs?

1056. Can process improvements lead to unfavorable variances?

1057. Did an existing competitor change strategy?

1058. Are data elements reconcilable between internal summary reports and reports forwarded to the stakeholders?

1059. Are indirect costs accumulated for comparison with the corresponding budgets?

1060. Budget versus actual. how does the monthly budget compare to actual experience?

1061. How are variances affected by multiple material and labor categories?

1062. Are management actions taken to reduce indirect costs when there are significant adverse variances?

1063. Are there externalities from having some customers, even if they are unprofitable in the short run?

1064. Are the requirements for all items of overhead established by rational, traceable processes?

1065. What is exceptional?

1066. Contract line items and end items?

1067. Who are responsible for the establishment of budgets and assignment of resources for overhead performance?

4.3 Earned Value Status: Workload Security Capabilities

1068. What is the unit of forecast value?

1069. If earned value management (EVM) is so good in determining the true status of a Workload Security Capabilities project and Workload Security Capabilities project its completion, why is it that hardly any one uses it in information systems related Workload Security Capabilities projects?

1070. Are you hitting your Workload Security Capabilities projects targets?

1071. Earned value can be used in almost any Workload Security Capabilities project situation and in almost any Workload Security Capabilities project environment. it may be used on large Workload Security Capabilities projects, medium sized Workload Security Capabilities projects, tiny Workload Security Capabilities projects (in cut-down form), complex and simple Workload Security Capabilities projects and in any market sector. some people, of course, know all about earned value, they have used it for years - but perhaps not as effectively as they could have?

1072. Where are your problem areas?

1073. Verification is a process of ensuring that the developed system satisfies the stakeholders agreements and specifications; Are you building the product right? What do you verify?

1074. When is it going to finish?

1075. How does this compare with other Workload Security Capabilities projects?

1076. Where is evidence-based earned value in your organization reported?

1077. Validation is a process of ensuring that the developed system will actually achieve the stakeholders desired outcomes; Are you building the right product? What do you validate?

1078. How much is it going to cost by the finish?

4.4 Risk Audit: Workload Security Capabilities

1079. Are some people working on multiple Workload Security Capabilities projects?

1080. Do you meet the legislative requirements (for example PAYG, super contributions) for paid employees?

1081. What events or circumstances could affect the achievement of your objectives?

1082. What does internal control mean in the context of the audit process?

1083. Are Workload Security Capabilities project requirements stable?

1084. Is a software Workload Security Capabilities project management tool available?

1085. For paid staff, does your organization comply with the minimum conditions for employment and/or the applicable modern award?

1086. Is your organization an exempt employer for payroll tax purposes?

1087. When your organization is entering into a major contract, does it seek legal advice?

1088. What are the risks that could stop you from

achieving your KPIs?

1089. Do staff understand the extent of duty of care?

1090. How do you compare to other jurisdictions when managing the risk of ....?

1091. What are the differences and similarities between strategic and operational risks in your organization?

1092. Have you worked with the customer in the past?

1093. The halo effect in business risk audits: can strategic risk assessment bias auditor judgment about accounting details?

1094. Do you have an understanding of insurance claims processes?

1095. How can the strategy fail/achieved?

1096. Are requirements fully understood by the team and customers?

1097. How do you govern assets?

4.5 Contractor Status Report: Workload Security Capabilities

1098. What was the final actual cost?

1099. What are the minimum and optimal bandwidth requirements for the proposed solution?

1100. If applicable; describe your standard schedule for new software version releases. Are new software version releases included in the standard maintenance plan?

1101. What process manages the contracts?

1102. What was the budget or estimated cost for your organizations services?

1103. What was the actual budget or estimated cost for your organizations services?

1104. Describe how often regular updates are made to the proposed solution. Are corresponding regular updates included in the standard maintenance plan?

1105. Who can list a Workload Security Capabilities project as organization experience, your organization or a previous employee of your organization?

1106. How long have you been using the services?

1107. Are there contractual transfer concerns?

1108. What was the overall budget or estimated cost?

1109. What is the average response time for answering a support call?

1110. How is risk transferred?

4.6 Formal Acceptance: Workload Security Capabilities

1111. Does it do what client said it would?

1112. What can you do better next time?

1113. What function(s) does it fill or meet?

1114. Do you perform formal acceptance or burn-in tests?

1115. Is formal acceptance of the Workload Security Capabilities project product documented and distributed?

1116. What was done right?

1117. Do you buy-in installation services?

1118. What is the Acceptance Management Process?

1119. Was the Workload Security Capabilities project work done on time, within budget, and according to specification?

1120. General estimate of the costs and times to complete the Workload Security Capabilities project?

1121. How well did the team follow the methodology?

1122. Was the Workload Security Capabilities project goal achieved?

1123. Was business value realized?

1124. What are the requirements against which to test, Who will execute?

1125. Do you buy pre-configured systems or build your own configuration?

1126. Was the client satisfied with the Workload Security Capabilities project results?

1127. Did the Workload Security Capabilities project achieve its MOV?

1128. Was the sponsor/customer satisfied?

1129. Does it do what Workload Security Capabilities project team said it would?

1130. Have all comments been addressed?

5.0 Closing Process Group: Workload Security Capabilities

1131. How well did the chosen processes produce the expected results?

1132. Were cost budgets met?

1133. Were risks identified and mitigated?

1134. What areas were overlooked on this Workload Security Capabilities project?

1135. Mitigate. what will you do to minimize the impact should a risk event occur?

1136. Can the lesson learned be replicated?

1137. Does the close educate others to improve performance?

1138. Was the schedule met?

1139. Is this an updated Workload Security Capabilities project Proposal Document?

1140. What were things that you need to improve?

1141. If action is called for, what form should it take?

1142. Did the Workload Security Capabilities project team have the right skills?

1143. Is the Workload Security Capabilities project funded?

1144. Were the outcomes different from the already stated planned?

1145. Is this a follow-on to a previous Workload Security Capabilities project?

1146. How well did the chosen processes fit the needs of the Workload Security Capabilities project?

1147. What areas were overlooked on this Workload Security Capabilities project?

5.1 Procurement Audit: Workload Security Capabilities

1148. Is there a purchasing policy as to the amount of an order on which bidding is required?

1149. Are services/tasks combined in such a way that the market is used where relevant?

1150. Are criteria and sub-criteria set suitable to identify the tender that offers best value for money?

1151. Were the performance conditions under the contract comprehensive and unambiguous?

1152. Where an electronic auction was used to bid, were all required specifications given equally to tenderers?

1153. Do contracts contain regular reviews, targets and quality standards in order to assess suppliers performance?

1154. Was a sufficient competitive environment created?

1155. Did the contracting authority verify compliance with the basic requirements of the competition?

1156. Access to data, including standing data, and the identification of restriction levels and authorised personnel was in place?

1157. Are bank accounts reconciled by an individual independent of the disbursement responsibilities?

1158. What are your procurement processes with contractors?

1159. Are proper financing arrangements taken?

1160. Is the departments procurement function/unit well organized?

1161. Are there mechanisms for evaluating the departments suppliers performance in relation to prices, quality, delivery and innovation?

1162. Did your organization state the minimum requirements to be met by the variants in the tender documents?

1163. Are rules in automatic disbursement programs adequate to prevent duplicate payment of invoices?

1164. Have late payment interests been rewarded and could they have been avoided?

1165. Did the chosen procedure ensure fair competition and transparency?

1166. Are outsourcing and Public Private Partnerships considered as alternatives to in-house work?

1167. If information was withheld, was there reasonable justification for this decision?

5.2 Contract Close-Out: Workload Security Capabilities

1168. How is the contracting office notified of the automatic contract close-out?

1169. Parties: who is involved?

1170. How does it work?

1171. Change in attitude or behavior?

1172. Change in knowledge?

1173. What happens to the recipient of services?

1174. Are the signers the authorized officials?

1175. Was the contract complete without requiring numerous changes and revisions?

1176. Change in circumstances?

1177. Was the contract sufficiently clear so as not to result in numerous disputes and misunderstandings?

1178. What is capture management?

1179. Has each contract been audited to verify acceptance and delivery?

1180. Have all contracts been completed?

1181. Why Outsource?

1182. Have all contract records been included in the Workload Security Capabilities project archives?

1183. Was the contract type appropriate?

1184. Have all contracts been closed?

1185. Have all acceptance criteria been met prior to final payment to contractors?

1186. Parties: Authorized?

1187. How/when used ?

5.3 Project or Phase Close-Out: Workload Security Capabilities

1188. What are they?

1189. What are the marketing communication needs for each stakeholder?

1190. What information is each stakeholder group interested in?

1191. What is a Risk Management Process?

1192. What was expected from each stakeholder?

1193. Does the lesson describe a function that would be done differently the next time?

1194. Did the delivered product meet the specified requirements and goals of the Workload Security Capabilities project?

1195. What were the actual outcomes?

1196. Planned completion date?

1197. Planned remaining costs?

1198. Who controlled key decisions that were made?

1199. What is the information level of detail required for each stakeholder?

1200. What could be done to improve the process?

1201. What is in it for you?

1202. Were messages directly related to the release strategy or phases of the Workload Security Capabilities project?

1203. Does the lesson educate others to improve performance?

1204. In addition to assessing whether the Workload Security Capabilities project was successful, it is equally critical to analyze why it was or was not fully successful. Are you including this?

5.4 Lessons Learned: Workload Security Capabilities

1205. What did you put in place to ensure success?

1206. If issue escalation was required, how effectively were issues resolved?

1207. What are the Benefits of Measurements?

1208. How much time is required for the task?

1209. How much communication is task-related?

1210. What is the growth stage of your organization?

1211. Were the Workload Security Capabilities project objectives met (if not, briefly account for what wasnt met)?

1212. What is your working hypothesis, if you have one?

1213. Would you spend your own time fixing this issue?

1214. What are the internal dependencies?

1215. What are the external dependencies?

1216. Was the user/client satisfied with the end product?

1217. What is your organizational ideology?

1218. How effective was the architecture/system design process?

1219. How often do communications get lost?

1220. What is the supervisor to staff ratio?

1221. Why do you need to measure?

1222. What was helpful to know when planning the deployment?

1223. How many interest groups are stakeholders?

1224. Were the aims and objectives achieved?

Index

impacts   49, 57, 134, 172
implement   54, 68, 91
implicit 117
importance   234
important   17, 24, 38, 59-60, 108, 110, 113-114, 118, 122, 128,
135, 147, 168, 186, 217, 234, 242
improve   2, 10, 62, 74-76, 78-80, 84-88, 168, 186, 208, 235,
253, 260
improved   82, 88-89, 100, 210
improves   129
improving   82, 218
inaccurate   141
inadequate   202
incentives   92
incident   201
include   80, 142, 156, 176-177, 190, 194, 210
included   2, 8, 23, 49, 143, 149, 157, 172, 179-180, 249, 258
INCLUDES   10
including   27, 31, 36, 43, 50-51, 75, 92, 98, 226, 255, 260
incomplete   141
increase   84, 125, 149, 184
increased   113, 192
increasing   105, 225
incurred   46
incurring   154
in-depth   9, 11
indicate   71, 92, 111
indicated   99
indicators   20, 48, 57, 59-60, 65, 70, 89, 92
indirect   55, 154-155, 178-179, 190, 244
indirectly   1
individual   1, 48, 128, 156, 159, 231, 234, 236, 256
industries   202
industry   95, 115, 118, 226
infinite 117
influence   76, 106, 132, 192, 196-197, 224-225, 236
influences   134
informal   242
informed   106
ingrained   101
inherent   114, 193
in-house   256
initial   111

protection   115
provide   112, 125, 132, 137, 143, 154, 165, 172, 179-180,
234, 241, 243
provided   12, 96, 177, 228
providers   84, 209
provides   144, 162, 168, 226
providing   97, 132, 162
provision   224
provokes   215
Public 256
published   214
publisher   1
pulled 112
purchase   8
purchasing   255
purpose   2, 10, 111, 168, 180, 182, 188, 231, 236, 240-242
purposes   137, 247
pushing   115
qualified   36, 59, 63-65, 148
qualifies   63, 70
qualify 57, 67
qualities   22
quality 1, 4, 6, 10, 20, 45, 53, 56, 62, 64, 66, 81, 95, 99, 106, 136,
140, 147-148, 170-171, 175-176, 178, 182, 184, 186, 188-189, 194,
224, 226-227, 255-256
quantified   94
quantify   57
quantity   210
question   11, 16, 28, 44, 58, 74, 91, 104, 135, 188
questions   8-9, 11, 62, 172, 196, 226
quickly 10, 59, 68-69
radically   71
rather 106
rational   244
rationale   224
reached   23
reactivate   110
readiness   34
readings   100
realistic   23, 60, 118, 137, 204, 236
reality 157
realize 53
realized   252

social   119, 134
societal   116
software   22, 142, 149, 154, 199, 216, 247, 249
solicit   39, 232
solution   46, 62, 74-77, 80-83, 85, 87, 91, 147, 149, 249
solutions   44, 75, 77-78, 88, 97
solved 19
Someone   8
Sometimes   44
source 5, 125, 206, 209-210
sources   31, 58, 69, 202
special 31, 96, 210, 215
specific   9, 20, 36, 38, 41, 71, 118, 163, 166, 192, 202-204,
219, 223, 241
specified   243, 259
specify 154, 241
spoken 106
sponsor   24, 157, 217, 230, 252
sponsors   24, 179, 188, 233
spread 98, 102
stable   142, 198, 247
staffed 29
staffing 27, 92, 137
standard   8, 95-96, 166, 249
standards   1, 10-11, 94, 99, 101-102, 149, 186, 188-189, 209,
223, 255
standing   255
started 9
starting 10
startup 131
start-up   229
stated   121-122, 154, 190, 232, 254
statement   3, 11, 78, 81, 147, 154
statements   12, 27, 36, 43, 57, 61, 73, 90, 103, 126, 188
static   221
status   6-7, 67, 147, 194, 218, 230, 237, 243, 245, 249
statute 203
statutory   230
steady 52
Steering   149
stopper   143
storage   188, 227, 242
stored   141, 227

CPSIA information can be obtained
at www.ICGtesting.com
Printed in the USA
BVHW041010200819
556236BV00011B/710/P